Becoming Bridges

COWLEY PUBLICATIONS is a ministry of the brothers of the Society of Saint John the Evangelist, a monastic order in the Episcopal Church. Our mission is to provide books and resources for those seeking spiritual and theological formation. COWLEY PUBLICATIONS is committed to developing a new generation of writers and teachers who will encourage people to think and pray in new ways about spirituality, reconciliation, and the future.

Becoming Bridges
The Spirit and Practice of Diversity

by Gary Commins

Cowley Publications
CAMBRIDGE, MASSACHUSETTS

Published in the United States of America by Cowley Publications, a division of the Society of Saint John the Evangelist. No portion of this book may be reproduced, stored in or introduced into a retrieval system, or transmitted, in any form or by any means—including photocopying— without the prior written permission of Cowley Publications, except in the case of brief quotations embedded in critical articles and reviews.

Library of Congress Cataloging-in-Publication Data
Commins, Gary, 1952–
     Becoming bridges : the spirit and practice of diversity /
by Gary Commins
        p. cm.
     Includes bibliographical references.
     ISBN-13: 978-1-56101-294-7 (pbk. : alk. paper)
     ISBN-10: 1-56101-294-7 (pbk. : alk. paper)
     1. Church—Unity. 2. Christian sects. I. Title.

     BV601.5.C63 2007
     261.2—dc22
                                        2006026496

Scripture quotations are from the *New Revised Standard Version Bible,* copyright © 1989 by the Division of Christian Education of the National Council of the Churches of Christ in the USA. Used by permission.

Cover design: Rini Twait of Graphical Jazz, L.L.C.
Cover photo: Brand X Pictures, Jupiter Images
Interior design: Rachel Holscher

This book was printed in the United States of America on acid-free paper.

Cowley Publications
4 Brattle Street
Cambridge, Massachusetts 02138
800-225-1534 • www.cowley.org

To the people of St. Michael's, Isla Vista;
Holy Faith, Inglewood;
and St. Luke's, Long Beach

Contents

Acknowledgments

I WOULD like to thank the Episcopal Theological Seminary of the Southwest for the opportunity they gave me to be a Visiting Fellow in March 2005. What a gift of time and space and grace and hospitality! It was there that I had the chance to give birth to a first draft of this book. I would especially like to thank Charlie Cook, Paul Barton, and Nancy Busbey at ETSS, and Bill and Molly Bennett who first connected me to the seminary.

It is typically arrogant and always dangerous for a straight, white male to write about diversity. The twin temptations to project and to universalize from one's experience are among the great blind spots for someone like me. So I would like to thank a few friends and colleagues who have tried to help me to wise up here and there and now and then: Anna Olson, Winnie Varghese, Katie Derose, Jaime Edwards-Acton, Altagracia Perez, Carlos Alvarado, Lucky Altman, and Giles Asbury. They are in no way responsible for my blindness, but they deserve credit for improving my sight.

Books are not finished by authors but in a creative interaction with editors. I would like to thank Marcia Broucek and

Michael Wilt for the chance to work with them, for a very enjoyable collaboration, and for making this a better book.

Finally, I wish to thank the people of three churches in the Diocese of Los Angeles where I have had the honor and joy of serving as Vicar or Rector: St. Michael's, Isla Vista; Holy Faith, Inglewood; and St. Luke's, Long Beach. Each of these congregations, in its own way, taught me some of the lessons I needed to learn in order to write this book. I thank them for being my teachers and fellow travelers and for the journeys we have made and are making together. This book is dedicated to them.

Introduction

I **WAS** making a routine hospital visit. Daniel Freeman Hospital was within easy walking distance from the church but, to save time on a busy day, I drove. It was a pleasant visit. My parishioner was healing, and I said a prayer. It was time to get back to church.

But on my way out of the lobby, a woman from the hospital staff stopped me. A patient had died. Because it was the Feast of St. Joseph (the Order of the Sisters that staffed the hospital), the entire pastoral staff was away at lunch. Would I be willing to go and pray with the family? I thought to myself, "Of course."

I followed her to a room where I met a black family. A man had died only a few minutes before. Two women and a teenage boy stood over his bed. They were crying, touching his face affectionately, holding his hand, and speaking quiet words of comfort to each other. We introduced ourselves and talked for a few minutes. I asked if they would like me to pray with them.

As I prayed in a style shaped by my Anglican tradition—one uninterrupted phrase after another in a form I had absorbed over many years from the collects of the Book of Common Prayer—they began to say "amen" and "yes, Jesus" at the end of each phrase. As an Anglo who had worked for several years in the predominantly African-American and Latino city of Inglewood, I recognized their style of prayer. In my religious upbringing, such interruptions were tantamount to applauding in the middle of a symphony. In their faith tradition, *not* to interject would be like leaving a call in mid-air without a response.

Listening to their more interactive style of praying, I altered the rhythm of my prayer to make space for their responses. I also lengthened my prayer from what I would have done, had we all been Episcopalians, to meet what I imagined would be their expectations and—at some level—their spiritual need. Stylistically, it was not like a prayer their pastor would have prayed; it was something spontaneously syncretistic. It would have been more pastoral had I been able to pray in the style of their religious tradition, for the style of a prayer, like its substance, is part of its content, the comfort it might bring partly based on the familiarity of the form. Our prayers create a spiritual home made up of familiar phrases and shared rhythms, and I tried to find at least a middle ground between their tradition and mine that would be close enough, comforting enough.

I visited with them for a short time afterward to see if they would receive ongoing pastoral care from their church. That was the end of our encounter—strangers from different Christian traditions and members of different races meeting at the moment of death.

A few months later, I told this story in a sermon. I asked the congregation if I should have prayed with these Christians from another denomination. Their nodding heads said "amen" and "yes, Jesus" in their constrained Anglican style. Then I asked if it would make a difference if the person who died were Jewish, or a Buddhist, or a Hindu, or a Muslim? Would it make a difference if the person who died were an agnostic or an atheist? If the family wanted me to pray with them, should I—should any Christian—do so? The silent assent was still there; a few heads nodded, the faces remained open as if to say, "Of course."

But a wide abyss still divides Christians: There is no "of course" when it comes to ministering to persons from the lesbian/gay community. Many religious communities still excommunicate gay and lesbian persons as if on the basis of a command from Jesus. Even at the point of death, prayers might be withheld; or, if offered, the lingering, bigoted assumption that gay and lesbian persons are under a more stern judgment might alter the prayer in ways that would be insulting and injurious.

And questions about race linger on. Barely two years ago, I was asked to return to the Inglewood Cemetery across the street from Daniel Freeman Hospital to preside at a graveside service for an Episcopalian. When I said that the cemetery was in my former parish and that my successor—a black Latina—could do the service, I was told that the family wanted a white male priest. I declined to do the service.

If the finality of death does not bring a spiritual sobriety to the things that separate us—religion, race, culture, class, gender, and sexual orientation—nothing will. If death does not make us ask ourselves about these divisions between us, nothing can.

There is something about the shared, universal human experience of death that brings a solemnity to our otherwise scattered and often shallow thoughts about people who are different from us. Death is a test of how we understand others. Who would we exclude from our prayers at the time of their death? Whose family would we not pray for? Having been scarred by grief ourselves, whose loved ones would we not understand as they mourned?

Death can reveal—or bridge—divisions. In the hadith

of Muhammad, it is told that, during a funeral procession, Muhammad stood as the bier passed by as a way of paying respect to the one who had died. Those around him, following his example, stood as well. Someone nearby wanted to tell him something he assumed the Prophet didn't know, perhaps to save Muhammad embarrassment—or to challenge the respectability of the Prophet's action.

"It was a Jew," the bystander said, implying that a Muslim ought to stand only for another member of the true faith.

Muhammad heard him, but he continued to stand and asked, "Isn't it a soul?"[1]

One has to wonder at the political, religious, and interpersonal impact if all Muslims believed this of Jews; if all Christians acted this way toward Muslims; if Buddhists and Hindus and Sikhs had this depth of respect for one another. One has to wonder how this story would be replayed if it were a person of another gender or race or sexual orientation. Who would we *not* stand for if their funeral procession passed by? Who is *not* a child of God? Who does *not* have a soul?

Human Bridges

Throughout history, there have been people who have explored deeply the meaning of the divisions among us, and who have always found a way through them. Muriel Lester was a great twentieth-century Christian who lived and worked with the poor in East London. She hosted Gandhi when he came to London and, in turn, was welcomed by him in India. She traveled the world in the cause of peace. During World War II, she was arrested for treason by the British government for promoting peace in a time of war.

A few years before, after the Japanese invasion of China in 1937, she walked through Shanghai in the aftermath of a battle between Japanese and Chinese armies. Packs of dogs moved through the city picking at the corpses lying in the streets. She wrote:

> I roamed about for an hour or two then I found myself in a part [of the battlefield] to which the dogs had not yet eaten their way. Chinese soldiers lay all over the ground. They lay as they had fallen as though asleep, arms flung out, hands relaxed, a peaceful look on their faces. I went from one to another, linking them in thought to their mothers, to their homes and to God.[2]

The soldiers were of a different race. They were male; she was female. In all probability, they did not share a common language. In all likelihood, they were not Christians. They did not share a commitment to Lester's core value of nonviolence. Most likely, they were conscripts and may not even have entertained the idea that they had a choice. They may *not* have had a choice. Undoubtedly, they had a very different life experience. Yet she related to them as people who had families and loved ones. Like her, just like her, they were children of God; they needed no more of a connection than that.

When Dorothy Day—in some ways an American soul mate of Lester—went to Lenin's tomb in the Soviet Union, she prayed for the long-dead revolutionary. It was a spiritual act that would probably have angered the atheist and, at the same time, given members of her rabidly anti-communist religious hierarchy indigestion. On another occasion, Day prayed for Karl Marx, who deemed religion the opiate of the people.[3]

Of course, Day did not share Marx's and Lenin's scathing views of organized religion; she remained an orthodox, theologically conservative Catholic, embracing traditional teachings and structures to inspire her radical way of life. Yet she shared many of their social values and their hopes for a new and more just social order. In her young adult experience in the 1920s and 1930s, it was the secular Left that seemed to her to embody the social values of Jesus, while church leaders were content to hobnob with those who intentionally, habitually, or inadvertently oppressed the poor. Day prayed for those who would not have wanted her prayers. Perhaps even more surprising, given her political views, she also prayed for wealthy industrialists who violently opposed social justice.[4]

One has to wonder what the religious, social, and political impact would be if others were able to bridge these abysses as did Day and Lester.

Barriers to Diversity

For people of faith, diversity is a spiritual exercise. Like any spiritual exercise, it can be as charged with anxiety as it is laced with hope, as fraught with fear as it is filled with idealism, as frozen by certainty as it is open to change.

It is obvious from our era's phenomenon of fundamentalism and fanaticism that there are passages in every faith's sacred scriptures and written traditions that feed and breed bigotry, hatred, and violence. If one brings fear, anxiety, bigotry, and malevolence to one's reading of scripture, one will find in scripture stories that nurture acrimony, conflict, and bloodshed. If one brings fear and anxiety and repression to one's faith and to one's understanding of God and neighbor, one will find support for one's bigotry.

For centuries, people have quoted the Bible to convince themselves that *others* will go to hell; that we can exclude *others* from our concern; that God does not love *others* as God loves us; that *others* are not saved. We can think, these people, whoever *they* are, do not believe what *we* believe; *they* do not live as *we* do; *they* do not share *our* sexual orientation; *they* do not share *our* values; *they* are of another race or culture; *they* practice our faith differently than *we* do.

Every religious tradition has the capacity to devolve, to

close in on itself like a butterfly folding itself back into a cocoon. Each faith has a capacity for conventionalism, rigidity, xenophobia, even the demonic. Some people in every religious tradition see the boundaries at the edge of their identity as borders upon which to build fortress walls from which they can announce mutually assured damnation.

They act according to their twisted faith. They act violently, often toward those who seemingly profess the same faith. Someone who considered himself a devout Hindu murdered Gandhi. Someone who considered himself a good Jew shot Yitzhak Rabin. When Martin Luther King, Jr. was killed, it pleased millions of American churchgoers.

At the same time, others find within their religious tradition the capacity for openness, respect, empathy, and compassion. For them, each border that separates one religious tradition or culture from another is more like a viscous membrane separating two cells. The fluids can mix without harming either entity. People know when they have crossed from one organism—one culture, one religion—into another; they know when they are no longer at home in their religious tradition or their culture, yet they can quell their fears when they realize that they are in someone else's home. It is still a safe, if unfamiliar, place.

Muriel Lester knew that the Chinese soldiers—different from her in so many ways—had homes. The knowledge that someone is at home in another religious tradition or culture helps us to understand that what we find foreign, others find familiar. What others find odd or unusual, we find to be the very sustenance of our lives. And if hospitality is shown to whoever is in the other's home, our fears can be transcended.

Awakening to Diversity

On the wall of my office hangs a calligraphy by Roy Parker, a member of the Order of Holy Cross, that quotes the Evening Gatha of Buddhism:

Let me respectfully
remind you:
Life & death
are of supreme importance.
Time passes swiftly by
&
opportunity is lost.
Each of us should strive
to awaken
Awaken,
Awaken,
Take heed.
Do not squander your life.[5]

It is not only death that can awaken us to the seriousness of life; it is *life*. Most of the time, in spite of our best intentions, we live in a state that Thomas Merton called the "half-tied vision of things,"[6] the half-baked, partially formed, easily distracted spirituality that is the norm of our lives. As Christians, we struggle to live up to and into the particulars of what it means to believe in, follow, and love Jesus. The gatha's reminder is a spiritual shout, a trumpet blaring at dawn to the spiritually slumbering: Awaken!

What does it mean to be awake? Different religious traditions offer disparate answers, yet there is almost always a shared subtext. There is a saying from the Hasidic tradition by Mordecai of Neskhizh: You are not worthy to be a *zaddik* (righteous person) until you can feel the pain of a woman in labor fifty miles away.[7] This is what it means to be fully alive: to be so aware of someone different from yourself (the saying, in its traditional sexist environment, was intended for a man) that you can feel a pain you cannot possibly experience physically. It is a step beyond the most mature kind of human empathy into imagination, identification, and participation. When "diversity" is seen merely as a cliché or an innovation, it loses this most basic and radical step, the step into and beyond compassion.

Such an awakening is at the root of diversity.

The Spirit of Diversity

Diversity has become a buzzword and a cliché at the beginning of the twenty-first century. As Dietrich Bonhoeffer once spoke of "cheap grace," so today there are many forms of cheap diversity. Many churches in California coin the term if they have two members under thirty or three persons of color in a congregation of three hundred. Large businesses tout the diversity of their work force—never mind that the CEOs are still predominantly white males. The city of Long Beach where I now serve touts its racial diversity; there is no racial majority. In truth, though, most neighborhoods are ghettoized, and the city's economic and political leadership is disproportionately white. Superficial claims of diversity are everywhere in Southern California. As national demographic shifts continue, and persons of color slowly become a majority of the population, such claims will become more common even in rural areas.

Diversity, however, is not a fad.

When we unearth the *spirit of diversity* that is already an intrinsic part of our faith, our scripture, and our tradition, we begin to understand that it is an essential part of our life. Much of this book will illuminate a *spirituality of diversity* that is found in Christian and other religious traditions. The multiple references to religious traditions beyond the Christian faith are not a matter of a *religious relativism* that denies the uniqueness of Christian faith. Rather, they are intended to show a *religious respect* that is the simple and logical step that both precedes and follows "love your neighbor as yourself." They are intended to acknowledge that every religious tradition contains within it wisdom, truth, and love.

My background with diversity has been grassroots within the context of racial awareness dialogues and in interfaith organizations, but most of all in the spiritual journeys of churches that practice diversity in sexual orientation and culture. It has been said that all systematic theology is autobiography in disguise. In these writings, there will be no such disguise. Whatever theories have developed from my experiences, they did not antedate those experiences; they have had to stand the test of experience; they have been inductive.

That is why I can say without hesitation that diversity is not a theological fad or an ideological gimmick or a product of pragmatic desperation. It is not something a few people have created from thin air to keep churches open in flagging denominations or to undermine our society's dominant culture. If our hearts are open to seeking God and to loving our neighbor, we will find that diversity is already part of our religious tradition. For those experienced or interested in diversity and perhaps even more so for those who are not, it is critical to find the spiritual roots of diversity with equality.

I am fortunate to have taken part in many formal and informal interfaith and multifaith dialogues. In most instances, the panelists are people who have scoured their scriptures for the stories and teachings that speak of hospitality and respect. Even more than being people who would seek this message, these are people who have already *found* in their scriptures and their religious traditions a deep sense of God's love that dismantles barriers. As the Epistle to the Ephesians says, Christ "has broken down the dividing wall, that is, the hostility between us" (2:14), Jews and Gentiles.

These early Christians were peoples of different faiths, philosophies, and values, peoples with stereotypes of each other, peoples who—prior to the Christian movement—had failed to come together as equals. Each could be welcomed into the other's camp under certain conditions and assimilated as long as they were willing to give up a portion, perhaps the heart, of their identity. The church Paul envisioned was one in which all gathered together as equals regardless of gender or social class, ethnicity or religious background.

Diversity and Equality

People of every faith *can* gather together to listen to one another with respect. But to encounter each other as equals is the challenge. In a way, diversity—religious or racial or cultural—is easy; it is equality that's hard.

That point was driven home to me when lay people from my former parish, Holy Faith, made a presentation on cultural diversity. The parish at the time was approximately 25 percent African American, 25 percent Latino, 20 percent West African, 20 percent Anglo, and 10 percent from the Caribbean. A young woman, born in Ecuador and educated in the U.S., had an assertive tone in her voice when she said, more than once, that at Holy Faith we came together as *equals*. The tendency in far too many diverse situations is for one group to dominate another. The tendency in far too many bilingual churches is for the English-speaking part of the congregation to control the power. Latinos are welcomed (sometimes) in church but excluded (often) from decision-making, from leadership roles, even from equal participation in the congregation. They are seen as long-term visitors, as if they had to carry a Green Card to the altar to prove their church membership. Likewise, gays and lesbians can be members of a church, but they are only half-welcomed.

The problem can be just as pronounced in interreligious settings. When Christians come together with people of other faiths, because of the dominance of Christians in American life, other faiths seem secondary. Rabbis are often the only non-Christians at interfaith gatherings. There may be *one* Buddhist or Muslim among many Christians. Respect may come easily, but equality is harder.

When a group of religious leaders in the city of Long

Beach met to discuss starting a multifaith exploration series, the representative from the Church of Jesus Christ Latter Day Saints (Mormons) said that they were not able to meet on Sunday afternoons. That was a day set aside for church and family. Others at the table shrugged and said that it was unfortunate—until a colleague held up a verbal mirror to the conversation. He pointed out that if the *rabbi* had said we couldn't meet on Saturdays, we would have honored his tradition. We should have the same respect for our Mormon colleague. Especially because I am, by my own biases, more interested in a dialogue with Muslims than Mormons, the point had escaped me. We needed to be equally inclusive of all.

The Practice of Diversity

When I designed a brief "welcome" statement for the Sunday bulletin at St. Luke's, a church where diversity had only in the previous decade become proactively encouraged (it had sometimes been reactively discouraged), I wrote that we welcomed everybody "equally." Whatever one's race, gender, sexual orientation, economic status, or religious background, you—whoever you are—are warmly welcome. Along with an already existing ground swell of sentiment and sermons and teaching and conversations with lay leaders, that statement sought to establish the *spirit* of diversity in the congregation as a norm. But if there was no *practice* to back it up—and that would be discovered immediately—it would be a meaningless, hypocritical conceit.

What does it mean to be a Christian—who believes Jesus is the way, the truth, and the life—and to respect the faith of a Hindu or a Muslim? What does it mean to seek social change so that a woman is always treated as an equal to a man? What does it mean for persons from two races to deeply listen to each other's experiences? What does it mean to enter into a dialogue or into a community in which each person is welcomed equally, not "regardless" of who they are but "because" they are children of God?

It is never enough to *think* that you live by a right spirit, or to *say* that you love God while harboring antipathy toward your neighbor. To do so, as John Climacus wrote, is like dreaming that you are running.[8] The right spirit must be practiced, embodied, incarnated. As Martin Buber wrote, the plowshare of our principles must dig into the hard soil of reality.[9] At the same time, the world—its institutions, including its religious institutions—is not a congenial place, malleable, and eager to be transformed by the slightest flick of an idealist's finger. It is hard soil indeed. Diversity is valuable work, critical work, rewarding work, wonderful work, but it is work.

When the work is long and frustrating and not particularly fruitful, we can wither like the plant in Jesus' parable that is overcome by the cares of this world (Mk 4:19). We can spring up with enthusiasm but shrivel like dry grass at the ongoing difficulty of embodying that way of life. This is what happens to idealists without roots, to over-eager converts almost desperate to show the fruits of their conversion. This is what happens to the newly aware white person who wants to prove to persons of color that s/he isn't like other whites, or the over-eager straight person who wants his/her gay/lesbian colleagues and friends to know that s/he accepts them. This is what happens to the Christian practically salivating to let persons of other faiths know that s/he has redefined—or watered down or discarded—his/her notions of salvation.

Part of living the mystery of diversity is to practice it in our lives as they are, not as we wish *they* might be, or as we wish *we* might be. The philosopher Gabriel Marcel said that life is not a problem to be solved but a mystery to be lived. This is true of diversity. Methods, manuals, and graphs can help in charting this previously uncharted terrain, giving us advice on how to intelligently and intentionally go about doing the work of diversity. But, above all, we need to enter into the mystery of diversity in its many dimensions—religious, racial, cultural, sexual, and social. To do so, each of us needs to look around and within to find the spiritual resources we need to practice it. We must be more aware of ourselves, more aware of our religious traditions, more awake to others, whoever they may be.

The Zen Buddhist tradition, far more than Western, post-Enlightenment Christianity, insists *ad nauseum* that we must practice our faith, and that the practice is where we exercise and strengthen our faith. Zen insists that thoughts, words, and creeds are veritably worthless unless they are enacted. A five-year-old, it is said, can understand how life ought to be lived, but even an eighty-year-old cannot practice it.[10]

The Christian tradition has its own emphasis on practice. The Epistle of James is filled with admonitions to control our actions and our words: to make sure we do not favor the rich over the poor; to avoid being judgmental; to explore the spiritual sources of interpersonal and social conflict. The Book of Proverbs, likewise, seeks to consider the myriad ways that Wisdom can be lived in our daily encounters. Like the Sermon on the Mount, these portions of the Bible relentlessly focus on actions as sacramental signs of our faith in a way that would seem to be congenial to the Buddhist tradition. The Book of Deuteronomy, with its majestic summing up of the covenant in the specific lived details of community life, might be understood from a Hindu perspective as an attempt of a community to embody the *dharma*, the universal moral laws. If obeyed, they lead in the *karma* of the universal design to spiritual and social harmony (blessing); if not heeded, they lead to dissonance (curse).

There are many times in the Gospels when Jesus sounded like a Zen master telling his disciples to practice what he was teaching them. He often praised people when they enacted the Kingdom of God in their lives. He told the lawyer who had heard the parable of the Good Samaritan—the one who showed mercy—to go and do likewise (Lk 10:37). He loved the rich young man enough to tell him the truth: that the only thing—the *only* thing!—he lacked in his relationship with God was to sell all he had and give it to the poor (Mk 10:21). Jesus lauded Zacchaeus for making amends for his corruption by repaying everyone he had cheated and giving half of his possessions to the poor (Lk 19:9–10). Jesus praised Martha's sister, Mary, for breaking through religious conventions that barred women from learning, as equals, at the feet of a rabbi (Lk 10:42). Jesus did not merely want his disciples and followers to listen to what he said. He wanted them to put it into practice in their daily lives. He told them time and again to "follow" him.

The Christian tradition has returned to the importance of practice again and again. Philipp Jakob Spener, a seventeenth-century Pietist, said that "study without piety is worthless. . . . [E]verything must be directed to the practice of faith and life."[11] In the fourth century, when two giants of Christian spirituality met, Evagrius beseeched Macarius, "Tell me a word so I may live." Macarius replied, "If I speak to you, will you listen and do it?"[12] This is what Jesus asks of us—even when diversity's demands make us uncomfortable; even when we find out that there is a cost.

The spirit of diversity has been part of our faith since its birth and, like most of the essentials of our faith, we need to practice what we believe and teach and preach.

Blessed by Diversity

When individuals, organizations, and congregations begin to contemplate becoming more diverse, they are often anxious. Sometimes churches are forced by demographics to become diverse, or it happens accidentally or unintentionally. Other congregations prefer to die when their neighborhood demographics change rather than to alter what they consider their unchangeable nature.

Diversity is a responsibility, but it does not have to be a burden. In truth, we are blessed by diversity and are impoverished without it. My experience serving for over a decade in a bilingual, multicultural church—and now in a church that has a large gay/lesbian population and is becoming bilingual—is that diversity is an incredible spiritual blessing.

Kathleen Norris, who writes in appropriately spare prose of life in the bleak plain states, says that just as God is found in the wide-open emptiness of the plains, so the city's "holiness is to be found in being open to humanity in all its diversity."[13] Norris draws our attention from the almost empty Dakota plains to a congested urban landscape where we find the same awe-inspiring work of the Creator's hand in the different shades of a multitude of human faces.

It is a primordial human experience to sense the divine in a sunrise or a sunset or the vastness of a starry night sky or in a long view from the hills looking down at the distant plains far away. Today and tomorrow, in our towns and suburbs and cities, it will become commonplace to experience the divine in our human diversity. Both are places, ways, and means through which we experience God.

A Note on Spiritual Practice

Because both the spirit and the practice of diversity are so important, each chapter in this book ends with a spiritual exercise, spiritual counsel, and spiritual practice.

- The Spiritual Exercise is intended to enable an active reflection on the content of the chapter.
- The Spiritual Counsel is made up of short quotations

to be meditated upon in the style of *lectio divina*. (For those unfamiliar with that practice, it means mulling over the words slowly as if they were pieces of hard candy in your mouth. Feel their texture. Ponder their dimensions. Taste them. Do not swallow too soon!)

- The Spiritual Practice is a way to embody new insights or learning, and to make even a tiny commitment to a real or symbolic change in lifestyle.

Absorption is more than intellectual assent. Pray the content. Practice the content. Make it incarnate in your life.

CHAPTER 1
We Drink from Our Own Wells

THE DOORBELL to the church office rang late one afternoon. No one else was in the building—a two-story house that had served as a rectory, now converted to offices—so I went down the stairs to answer the door. There stood a Latino man about twenty years old. With a few words of English scattered among many in Spanish, he asked for the bilingual person he had met at the church the day before. Normally, I would have politely asked him to come back the next day when someone could help him, but his transparent vulnerability and sincere desperation made me invite him in.

We went upstairs to my office, where I pulled out my Spanish-English dictionary. (I had been taking a Spanish class at the church for several months, but my learning curve was flat lining.) Sitting on opposite sides of the desk, we handed the dictionary back and forth, pointing to the words we wanted to communicate, enunciating them as if our mouths had been numbed with a local anesthetic. We told each other our names, and Julio explained why he was seeking help. He was not being paid at work; someone was taking advantage of his immigration status as an undocumented worker.

After passing the dictionary across the desk a few times, we started to laugh at ourselves, each of us limited to one language when we so badly needed two.

That afternoon we began a friendship forged by that goofy experience. As time passed, he helped our church start a ministry to the local Latino community by going door-to-door and inviting people to church. His sense of humor poked air holes in our linguistic wall. As he practiced his English, he called me "Daddy" instead of "Padre." In return, I called him "*mi hijo*" (my son). His English progressed much faster than my Spanish. In part, this may have been a matter of aptitude; or he may simply have been smarter than I was. It may also have been a product of need: Speaking Spanish would enhance my ministry, while learning English could mean his survival. I could pursue Spanish, knowing that if I failed, I could still lounge in the luxurious armchair of privilege.

Then again, those with less power are always the ones required to learn two languages, two ways of being: their own and that of those more powerful than themselves. I thought of the stories I had read of slaves in the ante-bellum South who knew the minds of their masters but, as a matter of spiritual survival, remained intentionally opaque to those who controlled the outward conditions of their lives.

Julio finally decided that it was more difficult to find the good life in the economic labyrinth of Los Angeles—starting at the bottom of a rungless ladder—than he had at first imagined, and he returned home to Guatemala. A few years later, two colleagues of mine ran into him in Guatemala, and somehow they realized they all knew me. They told me that a wistful look appeared in his eyes and a smile beamed across his face as he remembered our church and his friends. I get the same wistful feeling whenever I think of him.

I wish that all of my cross-cultural, interracial, and inter-religious experiences, all of my relationships with gay and lesbian persons, with women, with persons of other social classes, were as easy and as joyful as my friendship with Julio. But kindred spirits can be hard to find even in one's closest kinship group. Even so, my first meeting with Julio sheds some light on the practice of diversity.

Communication at the Borders

For starters, Julio and I needed a dictionary to communicate. Without it, we would never have been able to understand each other. But even knowing the vocabulary of another language does not convey the multitude of subtleties and connotations that can go with certain words and idiomatic expressions. Language is not only a means of communication, but also a system of symbols. Christian missionaries in the past, for example, were frustrated when they tried to translate the Bible and Christian theology into languages that had no word for "sin."

Each language system is held together in an internal coherence that is not always evident to one learning it as a second language. Our cultural and religious identities are almost always bound up with our language. Languages are contextualized and enculturated; words are made flesh—incarnate—in the natural flow of two or more people who fluently speak the same language and share the same inaudible subtext. Even had I been progressing more quickly in Spanish, Julio and I could not have even begun to find the right words for all of our experiences.

Even when people speak the same language, there are often roadblocks to clear communication. When I was in campus ministry, I used to take monthly walks with the rabbi from Hillel, one of my colleagues at the University Religious Center. As Steve and I walked, we would share personally and professionally, but just as often we would share our faith. Frequently in our conversations, one of us would describe an aspect of our faith tradition, and the other one would say, "We have something like that in our tradition, but it's not called *this*, it's called *that*." At other times, of course, we noted the disparities in our religious traditions, listening carefully and respectfully to the other while acknowledging, no, we don't agree. It was not a *dictionary* that we needed as much as a *glossary*, for each faith tradition has its own vocabulary for the mysteries of God and the conundrums of life. Each has its own ways of articulating the unspeakable celebration of the divine in the midst of the human.

Language is only one of the barriers to communication. In my first encounter with Julio, many other factors played a part in our awkward attempts at conversation. Age was one: I was twenty years older. Our backgrounds were another: My childhood in Los Angeles must have been vastly different from his in a small Guatemalan village.

Friendships, relationships, and conversations with people who are in other ways different from us require a kind of translation. My view of life, for example, is molded, in part, by being a man, a Christian, and an American; by being ordained in a religious institution in which ordained ministry is honored; by being middle class and straight; by a lifetime of good health with no physical disabilities. In other words, being *over-privileged*—often in ways that are almost meticulously hidden from me—shapes the way I experience and perceive the world.

Communication among peoples of different races, religions, cultures, genders, sexual orientations, and social classes requires a commitment to work harder than we would with someone of a similar background. Potential embarrassment is the constant companion of any conversation that involves diversity. If possible, such communications are best accompanied by laughter at our halting attempts to bridge barriers. Even when we share similar traditions, we may need a dictionary or a glossary or a history book—or perhaps only the commitment to listen long and hard and well to people whose experiences and whose perspectives on life are vastly different from ours.

I think of one of my best friends growing up. Even though we both attended UCLA, we started to see each other less often. When we did spend time together, however, there was the same closeness, the same history of friendship, the same web of relationships, much common memory, and a shared sense of humor. When I went away to seminary, we saw each other less frequently, and when we did, my friend, who was Jewish, asked me lots of questions about my faith and about what I was learning in seminary. I took it that he wondered if I thought Jews and Christians were equal in God's eyes.

One night when I was home from seminary, after we had gone out to dinner, we sat down in my parents' living room, and my friend seemed suddenly nervous. Clearly, he was trying to address something very serious, but I didn't have the foggiest idea what it was. Finally, I started to get his drift, but I didn't help him along.

"I'm gay," he said. I was the last of our mutual friends to hear it. He had delayed telling me because he thought my religious beliefs would make me more judgmental. I realized then that some of his questions the previous two years had been probes to see if I would condemn him; and I realized that some things I had said in the too-great-certainty of my young adulthood had fed his anxiety. We talked for quite a while that night. Some of what I said was true; almost all of it was trite. When I protested that we had been friends for twenty years, and that my knowing his sexual orientation wasn't going to change that, he pointed out that my image of him might change.

After he left, I struggled to think through how my thoughts about him affected the way I understood our friendship. At the same time, the distance and slight strain that had entered our friendship during the previous few years suddenly made perfect sense.

Whereas my conversation with Julio had moved us from awkwardness to comfort, this conversation made me feel that the solid ground I had assumed was the foundation of our friendship was, in reality, built on something akin to one of California's fault lines. Julio and I had been able to overcome our unease in part because we could tell that the other one was equally unsure.

While any dialogue, relationship, or friendship that reveals more of ourselves has the potential to make us uncomfortable, my friend was right: I did see him differently. He was still my friend, but now he was my friend who was gay. I saw him more fully. Truth be told, I was so worried about appearing to be homophobic—thus revealing my comparatively benign form of homophobia—that I was uncomfortable leaving anything unsaid. That compulsiveness, I think, probably disappointed him. I was uncomfortable, not because of him, but because of myself. Often the greatest barriers to the practice of diversity lie not in "the other," but within ourselves.

Exploring Your "Cell"

Healthy diversity cannot happen unless we know who we are. In order for a culturally diverse people to come together in genuine unity, for people belonging to a religiously diverse organization to come together as equals, for anyone to enter into a relationship with a person of another race, class, culture, or religion, we have to know ourselves. If we are going to be spiritually grounded as we take part in diversity, we need to engage in a careful introspection. We need to know who we are if we are going to have a chance to understand who someone else is. We need to know how our experiences have shaped us if we are going to begin to comprehend someone else's experiences.

When people are trained to become therapists, they are

required to enter therapy so they can become familiar with their own neuroses that may unconsciously direct or negatively impact the therapy they will provide. When people prepare to become social workers, they are encouraged to "interview" themselves first so that they may uncover their own social location, their unspoken values, worldview, and biases that could slant or distort their work. When people wish to learn the art of spiritual direction they must first find a spiritual director and receive direction before daring to tamper with another person's spiritual life.

There is a saying from the fourth-century Desert Christians that in your cell you can find the pillar of cloud and the furnace of Babylon.[1] A Desert Christian's "cell," or dwelling place, was often a shallow cave or an alcove nature had carved out of a hillside with a small area in front for a garden. In this small space, the saying insists, one can find a pillar of cloud and the furnace of Babylon.

The pillar of cloud was the sign of God's presence to Israelite slaves fleeing from Egyptian soldiers as they trekked toward the Red Sea. The pillar of cloud accompanied the people as they wandered through the Wilderness and wondered whether God had abandoned them, bringing them out of slavery only to let them die in the barren desert. As a symbol of God's presence, the pillar of cloud—like any cloud—hid as much as it revealed. It was wild and unpredictable; it was God's presence manifestly with them, but also a part of God's infinite, murky mystery.

The furnace of Babylon was the place where three young men—Shadrach, Meschach, and Abednego—experienced the fury of the Babylonian king because they refused to serve the national gods. As the story goes in the Book of Daniel, the flames in the furnace did not harm them. So, while the furnace is a symbol of trials, tests, and suffering on the one hand, it is also a symbol of salvation.

To say that both of these complex divine symbols are

present in one's "cell" is astounding. It means that God's manifestation and God's mystery, along with trials, temptations, suffering, endurance, and concrete experiences of salvation, can be found in our normal daily existence. All that we need to know of God, and of ourselves in relationship to God and neighbor, is woven into the fabric of our everyday lives.

Exploring Your "Well"

Most of what we call "culture" is below the surface. We can see clothes, taste food, and hear music, but the unconscious assumptions and invisible values about touching, hospitality, privacy, physical distance, sexual taboos, parenting styles, what makes one "on time" or "late," and so much more—the truly critical and most powerful parts of culture—cannot be seen. At Holy Faith, I remember being frustrated at first when a Latino parishioner would say that s/he would attend a meeting and then not show up. One of my lay leaders corrected me, saying that in their culture it would be rude to turn down my invitation to come to an event, just as—to them—it was rude when they invited me to something and I said that I couldn't be there. Neither cultural expectation is correct on an absolute scale. Both are simply what we are used to. I have a preference for functional RSVPs. Others want to know that you *want* to be there more than whether or not you *can*.

It is important to recognize that there is no such thing as a disincarnate faith; there is no expression of faith that is not completely embedded in a *cultural* depiction of that faith. Belden Lane calls spirituality "the lived experience of theological insight within a selected cultural context."[2] In Lane's work, there is a strong sense of geo-piety, a spiritual tradition based on sacred places and specific landscapes. Mountains take a central role in Hebrew Scripture and the Gospel of Matthew. Fourth-century Christians who went to the desert sought to live their relationship with God in the context of "fierce landscapes."[3] The spirituality of people living in the Amazon would be expressed very differently from that of people living in the desert. One might suspect that there would be disparate attitudes toward rain as a sign of God's bounty. People in a rain forest would probably not be as elated about rain as were the people of biblical Israel living in a semi-arid environment.

Mountain spirituality is distinct from the spirituality of Kathleen Norris's plains of Dakota. Urban and rural experiences are completely different from each other and suburban spirituality distinct from both. Spirituality is a very personal thing, but as William Countryman has observed, "While there is an irreducible individuality to each person's spirituality, that individuality is, as it were, a variation on and recombination of themes offered by the social and cultural world that shapes the individual."[4]

In the 1980s, theologian Gustavo Gutierrez wrote *We Drink from Our Own Wells*,[5] a book based on the principle that each person from every culture has a particular way of accessing the divine that goes through—not around—our personal experience, social class, and culture. We often succumb to the common temptation to make a superficial comparison of our "well"—our faith, our culture—to another well, and to find value in our well because it is different from or better than another. The key, however, is to search our own well deeply and to find there what we need.

In the story of the Samaritan woman (Jn 4), Jesus initially asked the woman for water from the well of their common ancestor Jacob. Later, she asked him for the water of life that quenches all thirsts forever. We each need to know the answer to this question: *What is the living water in your well?*

What styles of worship and music stir your soul? What kind of sermon speaks to you? What liturgical language do you speak; which is your first religious language? Do you prefer to kneel or to stand during worship? Do you prefer a formal or an informal liturgy? Do you like formal "alleluias" or more emotive "hallelujahs"? Several bilingual Latinos have told me that they prefer to worship in Spanish because it is the language of their heart, the language in which they pray when they are alone.

Just as important as liturgy is how you relate to the Bible. Do you have favorite stories and phrases that serve as spiritual guides for you? Who are the characters in the Bible you identify with most closely? Are there particular insights into God or specific teachings or values that—for you—are the core around which all the others cluster?

Then there are the so-called secular things that are part of your "well," part of the living water that nurtures, strengthens, and blesses you. What do you read? What do you eat? How do you spend your free time? What are your hobbies? Do you like museums or concerts or sports or clothes or the arts? What kind of music do you listen to when you are alone? What authors do you like to read; what people do you like to see on television?

Knowing yourself is the first step in entering into diversity. This is only the beginning, but it is an important place to start. If you don't know yourself, you aren't going to know anybody else very accurately. You need to know what is in your well, what fills you with living water, what gives you life. You also need to understand that this is *your* well; it is not everyone's. The Bible passages you deem the most profound may not be the ones that speak most clearly to me. You should not try to force me to like what you enjoy or let me insist that you enjoy what I enjoy. Nor should you wait with a smug grin while I struggle for fifty years to arrive at your level of spiritual maturity! We each drink from our own wells.

Respecting Other Wells

In the musical *My Fair Lady*, Professor Henry Higgins, the ostensible mentor in the Pygmalion story who, in his mind, generously deigns to lift a young woman from the gutter, sings "Why Can't a Woman be More like a Man?" My experience in a multicultural congregation is that people from each culture sometimes assume, without malice, perhaps even intending charity, that *they*—whoever *they* are—would be better off if only *they* would become more like *us*—whoever *we* are. If only their values were more like ours, their children wouldn't turn out so wayward or so repressed. If only they valued family or education or the church as much as we do, their lives would be so much better. Why can't gays and lesbians be straight (some of my gay parishioners say, "We tried!")? Why can't Buddhists become Christians? Why can't the poor think more like the wealthy, or—to express the vantage point of people at Holy Faith—why can't the wealthy have greater empathy for the middle class and the poor? Something can certainly be said for asking people to be more considerate of a different experience of life or point of view, but it is a kind of spiritual exploitation and disrespect to think that everyone would be better off if they were more like us. It is always narcissistic. At its worst, it is oppressive.

Even if our wells were truly perfect and had universal applicability, the desire to impose our will on others would still be problematic. Even when what we have to offer to others is good and true and beautiful, there are intrinsic dangers in it.

In a short story by R. K. Narayan called "Such Perfection,"[6] a sculptor named Soma had spent five years perfecting a statue of Nataraja, a Hindu god that is the source of all movement in the cosmos, in whom creative and destructive impulses blur. Soma had created dozens of images before, but nothing this perfect. When he finished the statue, Soma looked at it and was overcome by the beauty of his work. He fell prostrate before it and prayed that it would reside in the village temple and "bless all human beings!"

While still in his home, he heard an intruder's voice say, "Never take this image out of this room. It is too perfect."

Soma ran and grabbed the stranger by the throat, but the man insisted, "Such perfection is not for mortals."

When the people of the village heard about the image Soma had made, they were filled with anxiety. Soma went to the priest and asked when he could have the image of Nataraja consecrated, but the priest wanted to see it first. When he saw it, the priest said, "This perfection, this god, is not for mortal eyes. He will blind us. At the first chant of prayer before him, he will dance . . . and we shall be wiped out." The priest said that all Soma had to do was to take his chisel and break a little toe on the image, and it would be safe. Soma, indignant, replied that he would rather crack the priest's skull. Chip even "a small finger," another leading citizen advised, but Soma was too pleased with the perfection of his work to consider damaging it.

The rejected sculptor resolved to make a temple for his sculpture of Nataraja in his own home, and he announced that he would have it consecrated at the full moon. When the full moon came, a crowd arrived from nearby villages. The streets were crowded. People chanted hymns. Children shouted joyfully. The scent of flowers and incense filled the air. When the screen that covered the image parted, awe hushed the crowd. Nataraja's eyes lit up. The god started to dance and to destroy the universe. Creation and Dissolution were one. The moon dimmed. The wind blew. Thunder roared. Fire poured down from the sky. A haystack was set ablaze. People panicked. Lightning struck the earth at random. People wailed. A flood came pouring down and waters filled the streets.

The next day, people came to Soma and asked him if he knew how many lives had been lost in the storm. They cried out, "Save us, the image is too perfect." But Soma would rather that "the whole world burn" than mar the god's image. For a brief moment, he thought about taking his chisel to Nataraja's toe, but he couldn't do it. At his refusal, the winds began to shriek once again. Trees trembled. People ran amok. Soma hurried home in time to see a tree crash on his roof. He picked up Nataraja from the splinters all around it. The image was unhurt—except for a little toe that had been severed by the falling tree.

At the next full moon, the image was properly installed at the temple. Soma was honored and rewarded for his artistry. He lived to be ninety-five, but he never used his chisel again.

Even if our insights are brilliantly true, even if we are filled with the best of intentions, the world cannot contain perfection. Yet most of our disagreements come less from too much perfection than too much insecurity.

When I was a child, my grandfather and his brother-in-law used to argue about who was taller. Both were 5'3". The adults would laugh, and the children would look on perplexed when one would say, "If I were as short as you, I'd never walk out my front door!" The other would reply, "If I were as short as you, I'd jump off a bridge!"

The moral I draw from that memory today is that the smaller we are spiritually, the greater is our need to feel that we are bigger or better than someone else, and the more desperate we are to put someone else down. It is our insecurity and our anxiety that make us want to enforce conformity on others.

In the Gospel of John, one of the people who personified conformity, who believed that everyone needed to drink from the same well—the one he controlled—was Caiaphas the high priest, who presided at the council that condemned Jesus to death. Caiaphas was the ultimate company man, except that his "company" was institutional religion. He believed that Jesus, along with everyone else, ought to mold his practice of faith to that of the priesthood that Caiaphas knew with unyielding clarity was best. Those who did not do so shook the foundations of the social order and of religion as he knew it, and Caiaphas concluded, "It is better for you to have one man die than to have the whole nation destroyed" (Jn 11:50).

Caiaphas did not stand alone. Those from other sectors in the religious landscape of first-century Palestine, such as the Pharisees, had become a whited sepulcher, beautiful on the outside, but no more than a container of decay and dead bones (Mt 23:27).

When we elevate the importance of our well, our way of life, to an absolute, we take a step down a slippery path that always causes or preserves death, instead of bringing life.

"Give Yourself to the Winds"

A nineteenth-century dervish teacher in North Africa, Awad Afifi, shared a story with his pupils that, like any good story pregnant with meaning, applies to the spiritual path to and through diversity.[7]

The rain started to create a trickling stream in the mountains. As the skies poured more rain, swift currents formed and ran down the mountainside, running through fields, past rocks and trees. The water moved naturally, easily, without intention or effort. Finally, it made its way to the edge of a great desert. The water expected to cross this as easily as it had the fields and rocks and trees, but as quickly as its waves splashed on the edge of the desert, they disappeared into the sand. Soon the stream heard a voice whispering, as if from the desert itself: "The wind crosses the desert, so can the stream." But the stream knew that only the wind could fly.

"You have to let the wind carry you," the voice said. "You have to let it absorb you." The stream could not accept this. It refused to lose its identity or abandon its individuality. If it stopped being a stream, how could it become a stream again?

"Why can't I remain the same stream that I am?" the water cried.

"You can never remain what you are," came the answer. "Either you become a swamp or you give yourself to the winds." After a long silence, the stream recalled how water conquers only by yielding, by flowing around obstacles, or by turning to steam when threatened by fire. From the depths of that silence, the stream raised its vapors to the welcoming arms of the wind and was borne upward, carried easily on a great cloud over the wide desert.

Approaching majestic mountains on the far side of the desert in the form of a cloud, the stream began once again to fall as light rain, trickling down slopes, increasing in strength, until it formed into the headwaters of a new stream.

Awad Afifi leaves the meaning of the story to the listener, but it has a message for us. In the practice of diversity, we need to let go of some of the things that we consider essential to our spiritual well-being in order to discover that we can still be ourselves, although in a new way in a new place, after we have taken the journey. We will be ourselves, but we will be different selves, less insistent that our way is the only way. As Jesus said tersely, "Those who want to save their life will lose it, and those who lose their life for my sake, and for the sake of the gospel, will save it" (Mk 8:35). We will certainly have to lose our self-righteousness and our self-interest. We will also leave behind part of our self-image but, in turn, be rewarded with a broader perspective of our identity.

In his famous meditation on love in 1 Corinthians, Paul says, love "does not insist on its own way" (13:5). This has a powerful message for us even as we value our *cell* and our *well*. What does it mean in an interfaith dialogue that love does not insist on its own way? Does that mean that love does not insist that a Hindu become a Christian? What does love mean in a bilingual congregation? Does this mean that love does not insist that people from different cultures adopt the manners of an English-speaking church? Does this mean that Asians and Latinos and people of the African diaspora do not have to adopt white cultural norms or values? What does it mean in a church whose members belong to different social classes? Does this mean that rich and poor live as equals side-by-side in the same pews?

Albert Raboteau, reflecting on his experience as an African-American Roman Catholic, writes about the delicate balance of the personal and the communal, the particular and the universal.

[J]ust as the historical Jesus became [human] in a particular time and place, among a particular people, so the universal Christ must become incarnate in all races, cultures, and times, for there is no leap to a spurious, colorless universalism. Unless we recognize cultural particularism, universalism becomes another word for the cultural hegemony of the dominant group. . . . The Church does indeed transcend race, but only by including all races within its embrace as equally valuable children, whose differences and unique contributions help to build up the Body of Christ.[8]

Raboteau's message has been a hard one for the church, automatically and habitually dominated by one culture and class, to hear. Many Christians have an equally hard time hearing this message in a multifaith context—that members of all religions are "equally valuable children" of God. This equality does not negate the uniqueness of Christ, but rather places it respectfully alongside the uniqueness of other religious witnesses. This equality does not insist on its own way.

If it hasn't become clear already, it is easy to lose our spiritual balance while trying to practice diversity. It is especially easy, on the one hand, to become disillusioned with our own limitations and failures or, on the other hand, to become bloated with hubris if we think we are miles farther down the road than someone else. To remedy that, I often think of the spiritual guidance from Simha Bunam of Pzhysha, one of the Hasidic masters, who advised his disciples to put a piece of paper in each of their two pockets. On one should be written, "For my sake was the world created." On the other, "I am earth and ashes."[9] When we are overwhelmed by the task ahead or disappointed with ourselves because we have been timid or cowardly or have made mistakes or seen a prejudice surface, we can pull out the piece of paper that reminds us God created the world for our enjoyment. When we get overblown with success, real or imagined, we can pull out the piece of paper from the other pocket and remember that we are mortal, frail, and all too fallible.

Whatever our shortcomings and sins, it is a critical spiritual discipline to remember that God sees us with eschatological eyes, eyes looking back from the consummation of all God's dreams, with forgiveness. Near the end of the medieval classic *The Cloud of Unknowing*, the anonymous author says that God does not see "what you are . . . what you have been, but what you wish to be."[10] We need never be afraid that our sins and prejudices, our blindness, and half-hearted response to God's merciful call to new life will forever burden us. When God sees us, God sees what we want to become at the end of our journey. In wanting to become people who respect our neighbor as much as we respect ourselves, we have already given birth to that person.

Spiritual Exercise: My Well

In the story of Jesus and the Samaritan woman at Jacob's well, Jesus promised her life-giving, eternal water. Each of us has our own "well" through which we gain access to the life-giving water, the source of an abundant life, and the sustenance of our spiritual life and our very being.

What are the contents of your well? What are the religious, cultural, familial, personal, and spiritual things that help you to access the living water?

Consider the illustration below, and write in the words for the things that fill your well:

RELIGIOUS
- How do you worship?
- What parts of the service mean the most to you?
- What kind of church music touches your soul?
- Are there certain kinds of sermons that move you?
- Is there a particular liturgical style you prefer?
- Do you have a preferred posture in prayer?
- Do you have any favorite prayers or passages of scripture?
- Are there any visual or tactile experiences in worship that particularly move you?

SPIRITUAL
- What are the spiritual sources of abundant life for you?
- Do you have a practice of prayer or meditation? Do you use candles?
- Do you take part in Bible study either alone or in a group? Are there specific Bible stories or sayings that have a special place in your heart?
- Are there books, are there hymns, that have been formative in your life?
- How important a role does fellowship play in your life?
- Do you make time for silence?
- Do retreats, sunsets, or a walk at the beach or hiking in the mountains quench your spiritual thirst in some way?

CULTURAL
- Which aspects of your culture and/or heritage do you treasure?

MY WELL

Religious

_____
_____
_____
_____
_____
_____

Cultural

_____
_____
_____
_____
_____

Spiritual

_____
_____
_____
_____
_____

Familial

_____
_____
_____
_____

Personal

_____   _____
_____   _____
_____   _____

- What are the things from your culture (or other cultures you have adopted) that make your life more enjoyable? Does this include art, music, museums, books, sports, clothes, or food?
- Are your musical, literary, or cultural tastes primarily within one cultural tradition? If not, to which cultures do you feel attracted and in what ways?

FAMILIAL

- What family traditions are important to you?
- What lessons from your family of origin have you embraced as an adult?
- How is being a member of your family a ministry? How does your family minister to you?
- Which healthy roles in your extended family do you enjoy?
- Who are your friends and loved ones who have *become* family for you?
- Who are or were your mentors? Who are the people for whom you are a mentor?

PERSONAL

- What are the games, entertainment, leisure activities, hobbies, avocations, and forms of creativity you enjoy?
- What are your passions in life?
- What are your key commitments?
- With whom and to whom do you minister?
- What makes you feel spiritually and emotionally alive?
- What other things are life-giving for you?

Spiritual Counsel

Meditate on one of the following quotations each day during the next week. As you do so, ask yourself these questions:

- How does this touch my heart?
- How does it affect the way I wish to interact with people I meet, especially people of a different gender, sexual orientation, religion, or race?
- How does it help me see large groups of people, especially people of other nations, cultures, races, and religions?

"Jesus said to her, 'Everyone who drinks of this water will be thirsty again, but those who drink of the water that I will give them will never be thirsty. The water that I will give will become in them a spring of water gushing up to eternal life.' The woman said to him, 'Sir, give me this water, so that I may never be thirsty or have to keep coming here to draw water.'"—John 4:13–15

"Your cell contains the pillar of cloud and the furnace of Babylon."—Desert Christians

"It is not what you have been or what you are but who you wish to be that God sees with God's merciful eyes."—*The Cloud of Unknowing*

"Everyone must have two pockets, so that they can reach into one or the other, according to their needs. In the right pocket is to be the words, 'For my sake was the world created,' and in the left, 'I am dust and ashes.' "—Rabbi Bunam

"[Love] does not insist on its own way."—1 Corinthians 13:5

Spiritual Practice

- After you have completed the Well exercise, wait at least three days and then look at it again. Is there anything you would want to add? If you had to prioritize your well's contents, which things would be absolutely essential to living an abundant life and which things could you live without?

- Meet with someone you know who is different from you in some way: a person of another race, sexual orientation, social class, or religion. Invite him/her to do the spiritual exercise of "My Well." Then share your "wells" with each other, getting to know how you are similar and different.
- If you cannot meet with someone, think of a person. Which contents from your well do you think might also be in theirs? Which contents from their well might also be in yours? Are there any things you think are in their well that you would like to have in yours? Are there things that you are more comfortable keeping out of your well? Is there anything in their well that you think might give you spiritual indigestion? Are there any things in your well that might do the same to them? How do your well and theirs both reach down to the same source of living water? Can you be thankful that living water can come out of a well that is vastly different from yours?

CHAPTER 2
Feasting on the Word

Economic hardships and food shortages have forced a foreign people to leave their homeland and immigrate into your wealthier, more powerful country, a land of opportunity. They seem to practice no self-control; their birthrate soars. In some ways they accommodate themselves to your way of life in order to survive, but they insist on retaining their own identity, language, culture, and values, which you find abhorrent, disconcerting, or ridiculous. A national anxiety arises that these immigrants will never assimilate, that your economy may suffer, that they may steal jobs from your own people. A few of the immigrants rise to prominent positions in your society. Rumors about their promiscuity and general untrustworthiness circulate; the gossip is not substantiated, yet the pall of blame persists. Your leaders express public doubt as to whether you can count on their loyalty in times of war; they might side with a threatening enemy, or become a chronic source of internal disunity. So your government devises ways to control them, to maintain your people's dominant position, and to make certain that the immigrants know that your people will always be in charge. The immigrants will always be laborers, but never full citizens. If they become too

threatening, your government will take more proactive mea-
sures to ensure national security.

One could imagine that this scenario describes Latino immigrants who, for decades, have been welcomed sometimes
surreptitiously, sometimes openly, as workers, but never
granted citizenship.[1] Or it could be Japanese-American citizens who were put in concentration camps during World
War II. Or African immigrants whose numbers were severely
limited by racial quotas until immigration reforms in the
mid-sixties. Or Jews seeking refuge from Nazi persecution
in the thirties. Or any numbers of people from the south
or west of the United States. The Statue of Liberty, which
faces east from New York, has always been selective in who
has been welcomed and who has been turned away, and it
has never faced south or west. Frustrated by his experience
trying to enter the U.S., Nobel Prize winner Rabindranath
Tagore said, "Jesus could not get into America because, first
of all, he would not have the necessary money, and sec-
ondly, he would be an [Asian]."[2]

But the above scenario does not describe the U.S. or even
a modern phenomenon. It is the story of the Israelites at the
end of Genesis and the beginning of Exodus, told from the
perspective of the Egyptians.

What in American history has been called nativism—the
drive to keep America for those born in the U.S.—is not a
uniquely American occurrence. Similar sentiments spring
up in many nations, yet nativism has had a potent influence here. It has always been a burden to immigrants. In the
nineteenth century, nativism was directed against Roman
Catholics from Ireland and Italy; in the twentieth century,
against Jews. Today, it often targets Hindus, Buddhists,
Muslims, and sometimes Sikhs mistaken for Muslims. (After
9/11 there were tragic stories of Sikhs in the U.S. being killed
in misdirected vigilante retribution because people thought

they were Muslims.) The drive in California against bilingual education in the nineties had little to do with a thoughtful dialogue between competing theories of education. It was a gut-level rejection of pluralism on any terms but those dictated by the nativist majority. It would have been popular in Pharaoh's Egypt.

Perspective Is Everything

What a difference it makes if we hear the Israelite's story with an Egyptian "spin" instead of the more familiar perspective of the Hebrew Bible. Unlike the Israelites who celebrated God's acts to free them, the Egyptians were undoubtedly terrorized by the plagues and grief-stricken with their dead soldiers on the shores of the Red Sea.

Perspective is everything. Reflecting on the nature of poetry, Emily Dickinson wrote, "Tell all the Truth but tell it slant."[3] Poetry, by its very nature, tells the truth at an angle to capture our attention and engage our imagination. The Bible also tells the truth "slant," often more than one slant at a time, as if to let us know there is more than one way of describing the truth.

There are, for example, two primary creation stories, along with other accounts of creation, none of which mesh. There are distinctive traditions about the Exodus and Israel's early history. There are competing views of Israel's royal families, many ways to interpret its exile, contradictory interpretations of wisdom, and unrelenting and often bitter conflict among prophets, priests, sages, and kings. The four Gospels offer divergent slants on Jesus. Distinctive communities with particular spiritual quirks and pastoral needs led Paul to make apparently self-contradictory but equally assertive demands in different epistles because his readers had managed to distort their faith in ways that were polar opposites.

Just as the Bible is *told* from a variety of angles, it is also *read* from innumerable slants. Each of us brings with us to a reading or hearing of scripture our own unique experiences, the questions and convictions of our hearts forged in our "cell," the lifelong quest and daily experience of our life. Our slant is partially shaped by the religious tradition in which we were nurtured, but it is also shaped by our gender, our culture, our social class, our sexual orientation, and our experience.

All of these factors affect the way we read and hear any and every passage from the Bible. People in the Judaeo-Christian tradition, for example, see Isaac as the beloved child of Abraham and Sarah. People in the Islamic tradition strongly identify with Ishmael, Abraham's rejected child of Hagar the slave. An Anglo woman might identify with Sarah, while an African-American woman might see herself in the experience of Hagar. The way we read the same story will give it an entirely different bent, sometimes even an opposite meaning.

Whoever we are, when we read the scripture, we read it slant. Bigots will always find things in scripture to reinforce their bigotry. The fearful and violent will revel in stories of violence, damnation, and segregation because those stories reinforce their need to project their fear and hatred onto others. The temptation for citizens of the U.S., as Episcopal theologian William Stringfellow put it in intentionally awkward grammar, is to "read the Bible Americanly."[4]

Whoever we are, we will be drawn to certain passages of scripture and exaggerate their importance. Each and every religious tradition has the capacity for rigid fundamentalism and violent fanaticism, for paranoia and xenophobia; each tradition also has the capacity for openness and compassion, for understanding and respect. It depends on the reader's slant and openness of spirit.

A Delectable Feast

In 1984, Robert McAfee Brown published a book that invited upper-middle-class North American readers to explore the Bible by interpreting it through what he called "third-world eyes."[5] In it he tried to help first-world Christians understand that people from other parts of the globe, living in poverty and oppression, saw things in the Bible that middle-class North Americans were likely to miss. Our truth, like the truth for the people of Israel, is often a "tribal truth." While some theologians rightly call us to go beyond our "tribal gods," others point to a value in the particularity of our tribal truths. Walter Brueggemann writes that a tribal truth made David a hero-king.[6] Horatio Alger-like, David rose from being the obscure youngest son of a shepherd to become the leader of his people. The visceral element in David's tribal truth is absent from a more universal perspective. At the same time, the truth of one tribe is not the truth of all nations.

In the tenth-century, Symeon the New Theologian described scripture as a "delectable feast"[7]: a series of delicacies laid before us for our health and pleasure. Those who have trouble embracing certain portions of scripture might demur that some passages, some morsels, are an acquired taste or even poisonous. Other passages are best consumed, if at all, with something more palatable.

As a preacher, I have come to appreciate Symeon's insight about the delicious and sometimes knotty intricacies of the Bible. The Bible features the poetry of prophets and sages, stark realism about human nature and strange surrealism about the cosmos, letters to peculiar churches, apocalyptic visions, and the creative imagination of the parables of Jesus. The Bible also contains numerous stories astounding in their religious and cultural arrogance, their contempt for neighboring peoples, their utter disregard for women, and their apparent abhorrence of sexual acts that do not lead to procreation. Other stories ought to strike us mute in their stark and violent brutality, their prejudicial condemnations, or their callous disregard for human anguish.

Anglican priest Naim Ateek points out that it has become almost impossible for Palestinian Christians to read portions of Hebrew Scripture because they have been misused by Zionists to justify oppression and degradation.[8] Gay and lesbian persons have the same experience when they hear a selective literalism used to justify homophobia. Generations of the poor must be exhausted with the misuse of the quote from Jesus that we will always have the poor among us (ignoring his reference to the injunction in Deuteronomy 15:11 to respond generously to the poor). Scripture has also bequeathed us with unashamed reports thanking God for the destruction of enemies. Yet there is always a balancing perspective, an antithesis to the original thesis that creates a new synthesis.

A well-known Jewish midrash on the Exodus story tells that when Moses, Miriam, and the people celebrated their exhilarating escape from Pharaoh's army, the angels in heaven also started singing. God, who was weeping, immediately silenced the angels.

The angels asked God, "Why do you let Moses, Miriam, and the people sing and dance while you keep us from joining the celebration?"

God replied, "They were saved; they have the right to rejoice, but you must remember that the Egyptians are my children, too."[9]

This midrash balances the tribal truth with a universal perspective. Without undermining the ecstatic joy that became the foundation of Israel's faith, the midrash reminds us that the God of Israel is also the God of all. God can both take and transcend sides. God is personal and particular, and also universal.

While the Bible can be, and is often, misread and misrepresented, if we read it wisely and deeply, understand the context for the prejudice, oppression, and brutality, and taste each morsel thoughtfully—and in light of the rest of scripture—we may find what Symeon suggested: Scripture is a feast for those who hunger and thirst for righteousness.

Another Slant

In the city of Long Beach where I work, the city hall is a tall building near the ocean overlooking the downtown area. If one had an office in that building, it would be impossible *not* to physically "look down" at the city. I have often been struck that the recent gentrification downtown improves the view from the offices of city hall. Yet it does next to nothing to improve the lives of the people living within sight of that edifice who are all too often scarred by poverty, discrimination, and violence. Those working in city hall cannot see West Long Beach or North Long Beach, two areas of the city dominated by poverty.

There is a parallel in the way scripture has traditionally been interpreted. The dominant tradition of interpretation has been to read scripture from ivory towers and royal castles. Most theology and biblical interpretation has been written from the equivalent of the top floors of the city hall in Long Beach, as if it were only from that vantage point that one could see the universal truth.

The past few decades have given the church "new" points of view, as women and persons of color and gay/lesbian scholars, exegetes, theologians, and writers have offered their interpretations of scripture. An egalitarian, grassroots, from-the-ground-up reading of scripture has begun to proliferate. Writings from liberationist, international, and post-colonial perspectives offer different slants on scripture that could not be seen from the heights. Ironically, the bird's eye view is always an obscured view of scripture. Given these richly layered opportunities to read scripture in new and not-so-new ways, what would we find if we were to read scripture from the slant of diversity?

We can return to the Bible again and again without ever exhausting its ability to nourish us. As the twentieth-century Jewish scholar Gershom Scholem wrote, what makes the Bible extraordinary is not the straightforward meaning of its stories, but their "endless interpretability."[10] Because we change, because our consciousness shifts, because we outgrow some perspectives and open ourselves to new ones, because we find ourselves communicating in a completely different environment, we can always find yet another slant on the same story, the same verse, even the same word.

Each time I have moved to a new parish, I have found that it takes about a year to learn how to preach in the new church. This awareness was most acute when I went to Holy Faith in Inglewood and noticed that, as I looked at the same passages I had preached on in the past, I was finding things I had never seen before. My personal social class had not changed, but the social location of my ministry had. I had not been reading scripture with third-world eyes, or immigrant eyes, or inner-city eyes. My experiences with Holy Faith Church and that community tilted (or straightened out) my reading of scripture.

Having now served in four very different congregations, I have been blessed to be in congregations that have had their identity and vocation profoundly shaped by their social location and their geo-piety. In my university congregation, the focus was, naturally, on students and academic life. In such an environment, the Bible will say particular things to an intergenerational and intellectual church. In an urban, bilingual, multicultural congregation, where cultural catholicity is the centerpiece of its identity, scripture is read differently. When I was in a suburban congregation, the same passages spoke a completely different language. Now at St. Luke's in one of the most diverse cities in the U.S., those same passages offer yet another message.

One recent school of thought asserts that all theology is "local theology."[11] What we discover in our congregational life is only a partial truth, but it also contains something of infinite importance to contribute to the universal truth.

When I used to discuss portions of the Hebrew Bible with my rabbi colleague Steve, I was struck by how differently we interpreted the same passages. It was not only a matter of our personal differences. We are both part of religious communities that have treasured these stories for over two millennia. Each of us comes from a venerable tradition of interpreting scripture through the collective experience of our faith communities.

For me as a Christian, all scripture is interpreted through the lens of Christ and through the traditions of the church, as well as an unconscious tradition that remembers the days of persecution in the early church from the perspective of centuries of religious establishment and political ascendancy.

For Steve, as a Jew, the Hebrew Bible is interpreted through an equally venerable tradition of mishnah, Talmud, and midrash. It is heard through a history of oppression, dislocation, and mass murder. The Holocaust was only the pinnacle of horror in a long chronicle of persecutions and pogroms carried out by Christians who sometimes had the gall to invoke the name of a Jewish Jesus in carrying out their crimes.

No wonder we would read the same words from a different angle. Each of us reads the Bible as individuals shaped by our own experience, but we also read it in light of the experience of our religious culture.

The Struggle for Identity

The Bible is a very complicated and compelling story in which people wrestle with the meaning of both their religious identity and their religious vocation.

The first eleven chapters of Genesis record four "falls" or transgressions: Adam and Eve against God, Cain against Abel, the world of Noah's time against God and neighbor, and the people who build the Tower of Babel against God. The first three "falls" were mended. God repaired the first one physically by mending clothes for Adam and Eve as they left the garden so that they did not take their shame with them. Abel's death was mended when Cain was not punished with "an eye for an eye" but went into exile. Noah's flood ended with a majestic rainbow that declared God's deepened covenant with the world. But, as theologian Kosuke Koyama notes, after the fourth "fall," the story of Babel, there was "an explosive theological silence."[12]

This fragmentation, and the torturous, circuitous trail back to the reconciliation of all peoples with one another and with God, is a primary plot in scripture. God called Abraham and Sarah in response to the Tower of Babel and the balkanization of the human race. Through them and their physical and spiritual descendants, the human race was to be blessed, healed, and unified.

As the family history of Genesis gave way to the people's history in Exodus, it was the people of Israel who were to be a role model and a blessing to other nations. Others would see how the people of Israel lived. They would witness Israel's covenant with God, and be inspired because no other nation or people had such a profound knowledge of God (Deut 4:6–8). Then, either out of envy or because attracted to that way of life, others would come to Jerusalem—as the prophets later envisioned—to learn to live God's ways (Isa 2:2–4, Mic 4:2–4).

At Mount Sinai the people of Israel were given their first and clearest connection between their religious vocation and identity. Even as they received the first of hundreds of commandments, they were reminded of their experience in Egypt and the ways God's divine hand had brought them out of slavery. At the same time, they were given a vision of a land in which they would live with justice and generosity. They were given their vocation to be a nation of priests, intermediaries, between God and the other peoples of the earth, and their identity as God's people was renewed.

But as the people occupied the Promised Land, the tension

between this original vocation and the requirements of survival in a hostile environment became polar pulls in Israel's theology and life. When physical survival became paramount, anxiety flourished and anger grew. When the people were almost swallowed up culturally, when they were in exile or were an occupied colony in an empire, the struggle to maintain a religious identity conflicted with their original vocation.

As the story of this people continued, the struggle to hold their vocation and identity together became increasingly complicated in the harsh realities of a hostile world. A xenophobic nationalism colors the Book of Joshua as God directed the recently freed people to act like their oppressors in Egypt. They were told to defeat and decimate the peoples in Canaan as they put whole cities—men, women, and children—under what was called the "ban."

Though these writings reflect a later anxiety—after Israel had known defeat at the hands of its neighbors—and expressed Israel's impotent rage at being powerless against oppressive powers, this does little to alleviate the horror we feel in reading such stories. Their impotent fury is tersely expressed in the last verse of Psalm 137, an otherwise wistful prayer about the difficulty of praising God in exile, and the determination not to forget one's true home. It concludes, "Happy shall they be who take your little ones and dash them against the rock!"

In the Book of Judges, Israel's tribalism was taken to an extreme, leading the twelve tribes to turn on one another. When the tribes of Ephraim and Gilead battled each other at the fords of the River Jordan—symbol of the people's entry into the Promised Land—they tested the members of each tribe to see if they could say "Shibboleth." Those who said instead "Sibboleth" were to be killed (Judg 12:6). To have the wrong accent, in this instance, was not a matter of discrimination, but of life and death.

While we may want to shun such passages, what is admirable about Hebrew Scripture is that it never airbrushes its past. It portrays what theologian Justo Gonzalez calls a "non-innocent" history.[13] There is a remarkable honesty throughout Hebrew Scripture, a willingness to reveal Israel under the least flattering light.

While from the standpoint of diversity these are often the most unattractive portions of scripture, they make perfect sense. Fear, anxiety, and anger are typical responses of threatened, oppressed, and insecure peoples throughout history. When the people of biblical Israel saw neighboring religions as a temptation or as a threat to their covenantal relationship with God, they responded with rigid, harsh laws. It is no different in our time. When Native American peoples faced the dual destructive powers of domination and absorption, they strengthened their identity. Other people of color—of African, Asian, and Latino descent—have also fought to preserve their cultural and religious identity against the alluring siren's cry of assimilation.

The people of Israel were a small nation trying to nurture their religious identity while surrounded by often-hostile neighbors, and they expressed their fear of universalism in many ways. Knowing that they, as God's people, were not to be like the Egyptians, Canaanites, Babylonians, Samaritans, or any people who crossed their path, they sought to order themselves in ways that were at times exclusive and closed off from differences of any kind.

The "holiness code" of Leviticus is well-known for its culturally specific sensibilities and its sometimes downright oddities in defining the things that could exclude one from grace. Eating certain foods, wearing clothes made out of two kinds of fabric, some kinds of baldness, and engaging in various sexual practices (some of which may have been closely identified with neighboring cultures) could throw one out of a state of grace as surely as stealing or committing murder. As culturally conditioned as we may see it today, in its time it provided a way for the Israelites to maintain a cohesive identity.

On the other hand, there is no NIMBYism in Leviticus. The covenant directed people to be extraordinarily caring of widows, orphans, and non-citizens; laws were built into the social order to make sure that those who lost their livelihood and their property would have it returned to their families. There were limits on the practice of slavery to make it more humane (the thought of abolition having not yet occurred to the former slaves in Egypt). Yet women are excluded— without even conscious consideration—from the covenant and mainstream religious life. This peculiar mixture of exclusion and inclusion, rigidity and flexibility, is something that would remain a tension into the time of Jesus, and is yet to be resolved in the twenty-first-century church.

When Identity Yields to Inclusion

While there is much that we might describe as ultra-nationalism in biblical Israel's history, there are many stories that run counter to the prevailing tenor of exclusivity. In the midst of the books of Joshua, Judges, and 1 Samuel, the Book of Ruth stands not only as a story of women in a man's world, but also as a foretaste of the barriers that Jesus would eventually break.

Ruth was a Moabite; in other words, she was precisely the kind of woman that, according to the Book of Ezra (9:9–14), an Israelite was not supposed to marry. Yet this Moabite— whose people normally lived in open hostility with Israel (Amos 2:1–3)—showed greater loyalty to an Israelite and her God than any man. By the end of this story of her amazing fidelity, Ruth's mother-in-law, Naomi, was told that her (foreign) daughter-in-law was worth more to her—even in this sexist environment—than seven (Israelite) sons (4:15). Ruth also entered into the heart of Israelite tradition by becoming the mother of Jesse, who was the father of David, making this foreign "enemy" part of the lineage of Jesus.

The Book of Jonah, that great parable of a recalcitrant prophet, is another story that parodies the rigid exclusionary religious-political nationalism that sometimes enveloped Israel. Told by God to go to Nineveh, the capital of Assyria in the east, Jonah headed immediately in the opposite direction, to Tarshish in the west. Forced by storm and a personal exile in the belly of a fish to reconsider, Jonah reluctantly turned back to Nineveh and announced that in three days the city would be destroyed unless its people repented.

Prior to this, in all of prophetic literature, no prophet had ever succeeded in getting the people of Israel to repent. Yet Jonah, in contrast to his more motivated, articulate, and passionate fellow prophets, was successful!

But when the people of Nineveh repented, Jonah—in effect—shouted, "Goddamnit! God damn you, God!" To understand his reaction, we need to realize that, in Israel's memory and imagination, Assyria held a place approximately equivalent to Nazi Germany in the history of Western Civilization. Representing the voice of the people of Israel who would rather see their enemies destroyed than repent, Jonah raged against God. The book ends with God seeking to reason with Jonah, as if Israel's religious vocation were wrestling with its identity in its most exclusivist form.

The books of Jonah and Ruth typify the stories and visions that reshaped Israel's religious identity to fit its original vocation. If Jonah extended the reach of God's mercy, Ruth, by incorporating the Moabite woman into its covenant, altered the very nature of the community, making it forever more inclusive.

Even in the Books of Ezra and Nehemiah, when Israel needed to rebuild itself and reestablish its religious identity from the rubble of the exile, the stiffness of those boundaries was temporary. More intriguingly, the historical context of that rebirth was within the open-minded policies of Cyrus, the Persian Emperor who allowed exiles to return to

Jerusalem and rebuild their city and their temple. His toler-
ance of religious diversity (as long as it did not subvert his
political sway) stood in contrast to the Babylonian policy of
religious assimilation detailed in the stories of the Book of
Daniel. It also contrasted with what had developed within
Israel in the time of Ezra.

It is especially in Second and Third Isaiah (chapters 40–55
and 56–66) that we see the prophet cultivating a renewed
open-mindedness among the people of Israel toward the nations and toward internal diversity. The prophet Isaiah had
foreseen a time when God would say, "Blessed be Egypt my
people, and Assyria the work of my hands, and Israel my
heritage" (Isa 19:25), when the wolves of Israel's experience
would someday be blessed with the lambs. Yet at the exact
moment when Isaiah had his hands full convincing exiles
that their return to Jerusalem was possible, God had a new
message for the prophet: "It is too light a thing that you
should be my servant to raise up the tribes of Jacob and to
restore the survivors of Israel; I will give you as a light to
the nations, that my salvation may reach to the end of the
earth" (49:6).

It probably did not feel like "too light a thing" to Isaiah
to convince the people to return to Jerusalem, yet God de-
manded more.

Second Isaiah ends with an open and unconditional call:
"everyone who thirsts, come to the waters" (55:1). Third
Isaiah begins by announcing that those who had been excluded from the covenant, the sexually different and non-
citizens, would now be welcomed. Because these two groups
did not fit the dominant view of Israel's identity, they had
been outsiders. But they were no longer to be separate from
God's people. God promised eunuchs an inheritance better than children; God embraced foreigners who practiced
the faith of Israel and accepted their offerings equally, "for
my house shall be called a house of prayer for all peoples"

(56:3–7). Even more, God "who gathers outcasts" promised to "gather others to them" (56:8). God always seems to have new groups of "others" to include.

Breaking Down Barriers

In Hebrew and Christian scriptures, there are steps forward and back and sideways. The context for the New Testament is not so very different from Hebrew Scripture. Like biblical Israel, the new Christian community was fragile and vulnerable and tempted to establish its identity by excluding others.

The overall thrust of all scripture is toward the creation of a new people in which individual identity based on culture, class, language, gender and sexual orientation is incorporated into the whole body of believers to be a blessing to all. Scripture models for us the successful, if unfinished, wrestling with this tension, with the Gospels moving us toward an inclusive diversity in which all are equals in Christ.

In the Gospel stories, Jesus was constantly breaking down gender, cultural, ethnic, and religious barriers, finding people at the margins of his society and faith, and inviting them into its heart. He shocked his disciples by chatting at the well with a Samaritan woman; they were as scandalized by the fact that she was a woman as the fact that she was a Samaritan (Jn 4:27), with whom Jews had no dealings (4:9).

Mark and Matthew tell a similar story of a Syro-Phoenician or Canaanite woman who persuaded Jesus to heal her daughter (Mk 7:24–30, Mt 15:21–28). Her faith was as astonishing to Jesus' disciples as was the repentance and conversion of the city of Nineveh or the fidelity of Ruth the Moabite.

Jesus kept confounding the disciples and the people of his time. When a centurion sent emissaries to Jesus to see if he would heal the Roman soldier's servant, Jesus responded by loving the servant of his enemy, an instrument of Roman oppression against his people (Lk 7:1–10). Jesus went against social norms when he was summoned to heal the twelve-year-old daughter of Jairus, a leader of the synagogue, but first healed a woman who had been hemorrhaging for twelve years. Not only did Jesus give a lower-class woman priority over this leader, but by simply touching a woman who was bleeding, he flew in the face of Israelite law that would have pronounced him "unclean" because of this act. Only when the woman was healed did Jesus move on to raise Jairus's daughter from the dead (Mk 5:22–43).

Jesus' crucifixion, which in the dominant piety of our time has become a matter of personal salvation, has a more universal context in the New Testament. In the Gospel of John, Jesus said that when he would be lifted up on the cross, he would draw "all people" to himself (12:32). Similarly, the letter to the Ephesians speaks of Christ's blood as the instrument that breaks down the hostility that separates Jews from Gentiles (Eph 2:14). The cross ultimately bridges all of our class and cultural differences, reaching out to everyone regardless of their religious or cultural identity, offering an expansive salvation far richer than personal salvation alone.

Two New Testament passages that speak of Christ as a pre-existent co-creator with God push the Christian faith even further. The Prologue of John's Gospel says that "the world came into being through him," and "he came to what was his own" (Jn 1:10–11). The letter to the Colossians says, "in him all things in heaven and on earth were created. . . . He himself is before all things and in him all things hold together" (Col 1:16–17). As Isaiah rejoiced that people of different religious and national backgrounds would one day come together in peace, so Colossians insists that something of the divine character already exists in all things. There is a similar insight in Hinduism's Gita, where Krishna looks on all creatures equally. None are more or less dear to him because the seed of Krishna is found in every creature; Hindus see Krishna, as Christians see Christ, in every creature.[14]

When we read about Jesus from the slant of diversity, the nature of Jesus' ministry, the meaning of his crucifixion, and the presence of God's Word at creation—not at the periphery of our faith, but at its core—create a message about human diversity held together by divine unity.

But not all messages in the New Testament are so immediately alluring. In fact, some of Paul's language—such as that about circumcision—is embarrassing to contemporary Christians. Yet his words powerfully reworked the way people in his time interpreted religious, cultural, and sexual identity. When Paul wrote, "Circumcision is nothing, and uncircumcision is nothing," (1 Cor 7:19), he was making a profound statement that negated the importance of religious and cultural identity. Paul's essential message, as both a Jew and a Roman citizen, was that Christ broke down all barriers between peoples; that Jesus inaugurated new relationships that changed the way people related to one another—even the way they understood themselves. All that matters is our relationship with God through Christ. When we are baptized, we adopt and are adopted by a new identity that is in Christ, and our old identities, determined by religious affiliation, cultural tradition, social class, or gender identity, mean nothing: "There is no longer Jew or Greek, there is no longer slave or free, there is no longer male or female; for all of you are one in Christ Jesus" (Gal 3:27–28).

Applying the meaning of Paul's writings is critical work in a multicultural or an inclusive church. It is the ground for saying that we welcome everyone equally. It is the spiritual root of the practice that encourages unity in Christ in the midst of every form of diversity.

Enacting Equality

The Book of Acts highlights the tension among the followers of Jesus as they tried to apply their understanding of

Christ to the practice of their faith in a pluralistic environment. Just as Israel and the first-century church continued to re-examine their past to understand their present, just as they continued to create new stories to renew their identity, so are we called to revive our vocation as followers of Jesus and as people enflamed by the Holy Spirit.

Perhaps the most dramatic turning point for the early church was the occasion of Pentecost, where the Holy Spirit counteracted the balkanization that had taken place with the fall of the Tower of Babel. Pentecost is a story in which peoples of fourteen distinct backgrounds heard the Galileans speaking in each of their native languages: "in our own languages we hear them speaking about God's deeds of power" (Acts 2:11). This was not a Lingua Romana, a Lingua Americana, or a Lingua Esperanto imposed from above—either by empire or from heaven. It was God's Word communicated into the idioms of people's hearts. At Pentecost, the church was born in cultural diversity.

Yet the strain among Jewish Christians over how to be in relationship with Gentile converts continued in Acts. Peter, who had become a leader in the apostolic church but still followed Jewish custom, refused to be in table fellowship with Gentiles. Then he had a dream of foods traditionally considered unclean, but in his dream he heard, "What God has made clean, you must not call profane" (Acts 10:15). When he woke up and greeted visitors sent from the Gentile convert Cornelius, Peter realized that his dream was not merely about a revision of kosher law, but a new way to see the human race.

Peter's speech that followed his dream could very well be the foundation for a theology of inclusion: "In every nation anyone who fears [God] and does what is right is acceptable to [God]" (10:35). If the whole church were to take this seriously today, it would mean that atheists, agnostics, people who practice classical African and Native American religions, people of different denominations and sects and beliefs would not be judged according to their theological response to Jesus. Instead, we would discern (not judge) their relationship based on if they do justice, love kindness, and walk humbly with God (Mic 6:8).

If the message of Pentecost is that everyone can express their faith in the language of their heart, we have to ask ourselves, "Where is Pentecost in our midst?"

Doing the word is always more difficult than hearing it. As much as we would like to say that our churches are molded by the biblical story, they are just as often shaped by habits and values better explained sociologically than theologically. In living the struggle with diversity today, it is not enough to articulate or even to convince. People need to be converted.

Just as the Council in Jerusalem (Acts 15) addressed issues of inclusion, so churches today face the same debate. This struggle is nothing new. When I remind my parishioners that in England the "parish" is a neighborhood and not a building, conversion begins. The cultural diversity of a community becomes the cultural catholicity of a congregation, a local faith community embodying the universal in its particular place.

At both St. Luke's and Holy Faith, when we talked about starting a service in Spanish, people said, "Let's show hospitality by inviting Spanish-speakers to the English-language service!" I convinced one proponent of this approach, who was still making this argument after we started the service in Spanish, to attend the Spanish service to see how it felt. Coming from the British Isles, she believed that the Anglican tradition simply *had* to be expressed in English with prayers and hymns of a particular style. After she attended one service, she was converted. Experiencing linguistic exclusion unraveled her previous conviction. She became an advocate for the church being bilingual and, in spite of her linguistic limitations, an important bridge to new Spanish-speaking parishioners.

At St. Luke's, after an unsatisfying vestry meeting about moving toward becoming bilingual, vestry members suggested that I speak about *why* we ought to become bilingual. In honor of the Ten Commandments and of David Letterman, I offered ten reasons. The list is much more suggestive (and sometimes silly!) than exhaustive, and it was partly determined by the particulars of our parish history, but it was a start.

The first and foremost reason why we couldn't simply invite our Spanish-speaking neighbors to attend our English-language service was the story of Pentecost: people need to pray and to hear God's word in the language of their hearts.

Why become bilingual?

1. Pentecost. From its beginnings, the church has been multilingual and multicultural.
2. Biblical history. The Bible is a long story of the people of God overcoming sectarianism.
3. Jesus' warning. "Woe to you...[who] lock people out of the kingdom of heaven" (Mt 23:13).
4. The English Reformation. The chief purpose was to allow people to worship in their own language.
5. Anglican history. The Episcopal Church is committed to promoting both unity and diversity. This applies to culture and language as well as to theology.
6. Our neighborhood. The entire parish is our place of ministry.
7. Our church community. In the Diocese of Los Angeles, people worship in several languages every Sunday. We would be doing nothing new.
8. Church growth. Why would we not want another 25 or 50 or 100 people in church on Sundays?
9. "Jesus." When I was in seminary, I saw graffiti that said, "If Jesus was Jewish, why did he have a

Mexican name?" English-speakers have no special claim on Jesus.

10. Our welcome. The sign in front of St. Luke's says "All welcome." Either we mean to welcome "all," or we don't and we should change the sign.

There have been times at bilingual services when I have seen people from fifteen or more countries. We were, in our small way, part of that company gathered around the altar described in the Book of Revelation: people "from every nation, from all tribes and peoples and languages, standing before the throne" (Rev 7:9). In some ways, this is the fulfillment of the promise of Pentecost. At the end of Revelation, there is a new heaven and a new earth, a new Jerusalem, and "People will bring into it the glory and the honor of the nations" (Rev 21:26). Unlike the visions in Isaiah and Micah, the nations do not come to the new Jerusalem to learn. They come to *share* what they already know. At the heart of the city is a new garden, like the one in Eden.

This vision invites us today to imagine people of every religion gathered at the throne of God. This is what scripture looks like when we read it with eyes attuned to diversity. It is not a matter of picking and choosing the things most amenable to a particular ideology. It is more a *way* of reading and seeing that applies to all scripture and tradition. Once we start to see and hear messages about diversity here and there, we start to see and hear them everywhere.

Spiritual Exercise: My Lifeline

On the diagram below (or on a separate sheet of paper), create a "lifeline" for yourself, from birth to the present. Put markers indicating the major times in your life when you have been touched by diversity. Make a note for each about how you were affected. Consider these areas:

Religion
Race/Culture/Language
Gender
Social Class
Sexual Orientation

Depending on how detailed you want to be and how much time you want to give to this exercise, you might want to create a separate Lifeline for each category. Or choose the area(s) that you think is (are) the most important one(s) for you right now.

MY LIFELINE

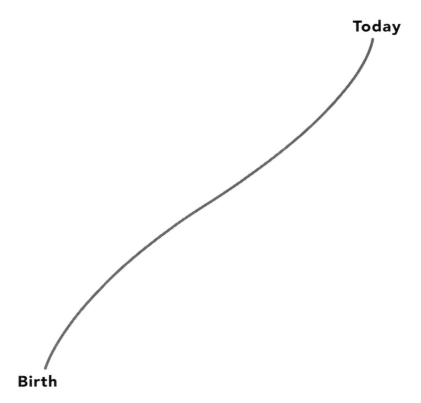

Spiritual Counsel

Meditate on one of the following quotations each day during the next week. As you do so, ask yourself these questions:

- How does this touch my heart?
- How does it affect the way I wish to interact with people I meet, especially people of a different gender, sexual orientation, religion, or race?
- How does it help me see large groups of people, especially people of other nations, cultures, races, and religions?

"In you all the families of the earth shall be blessed."—Genesis 12:3

"Love your neighbor as yourself."—Leviticus 19:18

"Blessed be Egypt my people, and Assyria the work of my hands, and Israel my heritage."—Isaiah 19:25

"What does the Lord require of you but to do justice, and to love kindness, and to walk humbly with your God?"—Micah 6:8

"Jesus said, 'Whoever does the will of God is my brother and sister and mother.' "—Mark 3:35

"Each one heard them speaking in the native language of each."—Acts 2:6

"God shows no partiality, but in every nation anyone who fears him and does what is right is acceptable to him."—Acts 10:34–35

"Circumcision is nothing, and uncircumcision is nothing."—1 Corinthians 7:19

"There is no longer Jew or Greek, there is no longer slave or free, there is no longer male and female; for all of you are one in Christ Jesus."—Galatians 3:28

Spiritual Practice

Choose one of the following for your practice this week:

- Prepare to read the front page of any newspaper (including the photos!) by reading one or more of the verses from the Spiritual Counsel above. Pray that you may see indications of stereotypes and systems of discrimination and oppression, as well as signs of hope.
- Prepare to watch television news by reading one or more of the verses from Spiritual Counsel. Pray that you may see and hear indications of stereotypes and systems of discrimination and oppression, as well as signs of transformation.

CHAPTER 3

But Now I See

ONLY A handful of students attended my elementary school on Jewish holidays because over 90 percent of the people in our neighborhood were Jewish. On these holidays there was no point in being at school. Yet we went. My younger brother came home from his first experience of school on a Jewish holiday and asked our parents, "Why is the whole world Jewish except us?"

It struck me that day as an incredibly naïve question. In retrospect, there may have been a wistfulness in his question that I missed: If we were Jewish, we wouldn't have had to go to school that day. Even though I was eight, I simply hadn't thought to ask. I had assumed that was the way the world was.

Our perceptions are shaped by our experiences. We tend to universalize our experiences—based on what we learn in childhood, from our family of origin, and the media—and project them onto the world. We make the world contort to fit the images that have accumulated in our minds. Yet like Paul, who said that when he was a child, he spoke and thought and reasoned like a child, when we become adults, we need to put our childish worldviews aside (1 Cor 13:11). As adults, we realize that what we thought the world was like when we were children created as much blindness as it did clarity. The associations we have with certain words, ideas, and peoples that were shaped while we are young can still mold our views of life. Unless something challenges those perceptions, they remain the lenses through which we experience the world.

Our stereotypes and prejudices are also formed at an early age. When you hear the words "Buddhist," "Muslim," or "fundamentalist," what associations or feelings do you have? There is an almost universal response that I encounter when I tell someone I am an Episcopalian. It is a perplexed shrug. There is no association! But for other words, other groups, other peoples, there are. What does a Buddhist look like? What does a Muslim believe? If you meet a fundamentalist, are you encountering someone with a closed mind? What is a lesbian like? Are rich people different from poor people? How? We all have set notions.

Much to the amusement of his fellow parishioners, a member of a search committee at an Episcopal church, a respected and beloved man in his early nineties, refused to interview a fifty-eight-year-old candidate for the position because, in his mind, the candidate was too old!

Annie Dillard has pointed out that we might think it hard to grapple with the reality of 1.2 billion (now more) Chinese. On the contrary, she tells us that it is easy: All we need to do is to take our singularity and complexity, multiply it by 1.2 billion, and we have it.[1] The exercise is both absurd and profound. It is a reminder of the importance of knowing our unconscious stereotypes of different groups. It is a way to diagnose our eyesight and our blindness so that we will know when we really are seeing.

Constructions of the Inner Eye

At the beginning of Ralph Ellison's classic novel *Invisible Man*, an African-American young man describes his experience:

I am an invisible man. . . . I am invisible, understand, simply because people refuse to see me. Like the bodiless heads you see sometimes in circus sideshows, it is as though I have been surrounded by mirrors of hard, distorting glass. When they approach me they see only my surroundings, themselves, or figments of their imagination—indeed, everything and anything except me. . . . That invisibility to which I refer occurs because of a peculiar disposition of the eyes of those with whom I come in contact. A matter of the construction of the inner eyes, those eyes with which they look through their physical eyes upon reality.[2]

James Baldwin said, similarly, that people never looked at him. He was at the mercy of their reflexes to the color of his skin.[3] As Ellison put it, the "inner eyes"—the universalization of our limited experiences, the figments of our imagination—determine what we see more than do our physical eyes.

I remember sharing with a group at St. Luke's something I had read in Gordon Allport's classic mid-twentieth-century book *The Nature of Prejudice*. A Jewish man said that antisemitism was always just "offstage," and you never knew when it was going to leap threateningly into your life.[4] A gay parishioner reacted immediately: "That's what it's like to be gay."

Living with such continual caution can make a person chronically wary or uneasy. Never knowing when someone, an apparently innocent passerby, is going to act out means living on constant alert. This was why light-skinned, mixed-raced African Americans sometimes chose to "pass"; this has been why many gay and lesbian persons have stayed in the closet. Who wants to live knowing that prejudice, bigotry, hatred, and violence may lunge out at you any minute of any day of your life?

Ellison's portrait of the invisible man is strikingly true. When we see a Muslim today, for example, we may see that person as a product of the "figments of [our] imagination." The Sikh man who became the target of vigilante retaliation after 9/11 fit someone's idea of what a Muslim supposedly looks like. When we see a gay or lesbian person—or if we are gay or lesbian—part of what we see is due to the distorting mirrors our society provides when it sums up what it is to be gay, another figment of our collective imagination. We see "everything and anything" but the real person in front of us. Because of what we project from our inner eyes through our physical eyes, reality remains invisible. This is the hardest kind of blindness to heal because we do not even recognize that we are blind.

A stereotype is a standardized, oversimplified mental picture that is pasted onto—or over—every member of a group. A friend of mine from West Virginia says that his hillbilly accent tells others that he is un- or under-educated. Some of my Latino parishioners complain that people stereotype them as unintelligent because of the way they speak English. In the Episcopal Church, having an English accent makes one seem more educated and sophisticated and—at least I believe; perhaps it is a stereotype—makes someone more likely to be elected a bishop or a dean of a cathedral. I have a friend who was born in Trinidad who says that when people see her, they think she's African American; when they hear her clipped Caribbean version of the Queen's English, they immediately replace one stereotype with another.

Stereotypes are often formed from one picture, one experience, or one projection. When I was in Junior High School, I played in a community basketball league. Our team won our league and went into the city playoffs. The first two games we had to play were against all-black teams; we were all-white . . . and it was the mid-sixties. We had stereotypes about who were the best basketball players, and they weren't us. But we were very competitive. Before the game, we talked about not being intimidated. And we weren't. We won two games and proceeded to a championship game in another part of the city. The team we played in the finals was all-Jewish. They beat us. The obvious lesson to extrapolate from this experience is that the best basketball players in America are Jewish!

Jesus quoted the prophet Isaiah who said that people had eyes that did not see and ears that did not hear (Mk 4:12, Isa 6:9–10). If we want to be healed of our blindness—and we need to be if we want to practice diversity—we must dig beneath our surface perceptions.

While *stereotypes* are standardized pictures that may be positive, negative, or plainly absurd, *prejudices* are instinctive responses that are built on the same superficial data. We may not want to absorb prejudices from our experience, family, and media, but it is almost impossible *not* to be influenced by them, to internalize them within ourselves and to externalize them onto others.

When I was at Holy Faith late one night, I was standing next to the driveway between the church and the office (there was no parking lot, so it had little traffic) when a sports car turned sharply at high speed into the driveway. It happened very quickly, but—in retrospect—I think I saw that the driver was black. I felt an adrenaline surge until the young African-American parishioner driving the car popped out of the door. Now it was no longer a black face that I saw, but a friendly face. A young African American driving a fast car late at night might be a threat; this young man wanting to show his new (used) car to his priest was a pleasure. I had to wonder: If I had thought the driver was white or Latino or Asian, would I have had the same visceral, gut-level, instinctive response? Maybe yes. Maybe no. Maybe similar, but not the same.

In *The Nature of Prejudice*, Allport makes a distinction between a *prejudice* and a *prejudgment* that hinges on a person's willingness to change. A person who has prejudged is able to alter the prejudgment when new facts present themselves. A person who clings to a bias in absolute disregard of further evidence remains prejudiced. Prejudice is based on deeply irrational (usually negative) feelings about oneself and an insecure need to lift oneself in one's opinion over others.

Allport gives an example from Rhodesia (before it was Zimbabwe) of a white man complaining that some African workers were "lazy savages." When they quickly moved heavy bags of grain from a truck, he concluded that they were "strong brutes."[5] He had new evidence that they weren't lazy, but still found a way to assert that they were less civilized and less intelligent.

Stereotypes and prejudices are pernicious forms of blindness that render us invisible and/or distorted to one another. They are the bane of diversity. We are blinded by what we think we see and what we think we know. We may be aware of ourselves and aware of the centrality of diversity in our religious tradition, yet this blindness may cripple us as well as those around us.

When the Humble Compete

There is an amusing episode in Yann Martel's novel *Life of Pi* where Pi, a teenager growing up in India, has decided to be a Hindu, a Muslim, *and* a Christian. When his secret is revealed, it upsets his parents as well as the priest, the imam, and the pandit. To Pi's horror, one day they all meet.

It is not that Pi's religiosity violates his family piety. His father is "as secular as ice cream"; yet, as the zoo director, Pi's father has newly arrived animals blessed in Hindu fashion because it is good for "public relations rather than personal salvation." Pi's mother's Hindu upbringing and Baptist education have left her "serenely impious." Pi notes that his mentor, Ravi, the other formative adult in his life, would be more impressed with religion if Lord Krishna or Jesus or Muhammad knew how to play cricket.

When Pi and his parents meet the three religious leaders, the priest insists that Pi is "a good Christian boy." The imam says, no, "He's a good Muslim boy. He comes without fail to Friday prayer, and his knowledge of the Holy Qur'an is coming along nicely." The pandit, in turn, insists that Pi is a good Hindu boy who comes to the temple and performs the appropriate rituals.

An argument ensues about the nature of the three religious traditions. The imam says that Hindus and Christians are idolaters because they have *many gods* (Muslims traditionally see the concept of Trinity as defying the doctrine of the unity of God). The priest asserts that salvation exists only in Jesus and tells the imam there is not a single miracle in the Muslim religion, asking him, "What kind of religion is that?"

The imam snaps back, "It isn't a circus with dead people jumping out of tombs all the time. . . . We Muslims stick to the essential miracle of existence. Birds flying, rain falling, crops growing—these are miracles enough for us." Christ, he continues, could have used such a miracle instead of being killed. "Muhammad," he argues, "brought us the word of God without any undignified nonsense and died at a ripe old age. . . . If the Prophet were alive, he would have some choice words for you!"

The priest replies, "Well, he's not! Christ is alive" while the Prophet is "dead, dead, dead!"

The pandit interrupts by asking Pi why he entertains these "*foreign* religions," implying that Hinduism and Indian nationalism fit together like hand and glove. The priest and imam, both Tamils like Pi, are horrified at such an argument. Besides, says the pandit, Muslims are "uncivilized."

"Says the slave-driver of the caste system," retorts the imam.

The priest throws in his opinion of Hindus: "They are golden calf lovers. They kneel before cows."

The pandit responds, "While Christians kneel before a white man! They are flunkies of a foreign god."

The imam adds his own critique of Christians: "They eat pigs and are cannibals."

All of this arguing leaves their faces flushed, and they seem on the verge of physical violence. When Pi's father interjects that India has freedom of religious practice, they scream in unison, "*Practice*—singular!" All three agree that Pi is a pious boy, but he can't be a Christian, a Muslim, *and* a Hindu. He has to choose.

When he is finally consulted, Pi makes this simple statement: "Bapu Gandhi said, 'All religions are true.' I just want to love God."

His thoroughly secularized father brings the argument to a close. No one, he says, should be faulted for wanting to love God. He has the last word: "Ice cream, anyone?"

Pi concludes, "That was my introduction to interfaith dialogue."[6]

The story demonstrates the ways that people use stereotypes, half-truths, and distortions to discredit others and to render the true virtues of other faiths and cultures invisible. The argument in *Life of Pi* over which religion is greatest is reminiscent of the story of Jesus' disciples' argument about which of them was the greatest (Mk 9:33–34). It is an odd argument, considering that all religions counsel humility. Jesus consistently said that the humble would be exalted and those who exalted themselves would be humbled (Lk 14:11). He counseled his followers to take the lowest place at a banquet rather than to presume they should have a seat of honor (Lk 14:7f).

One wonders how Paul's statement that love "does not insist on its own way" (1 Cor 13:5) would apply to the argument among the priest, the imam, and the pandit. Historically,

Christians have an almost automatic reflex that keeps us from differentiating between Jesus as "the Way" and our-own-way-of-believing-in-him as the Way. So the argument in *Life of Pi* is one that has often led to discrimination and persecution—even internally within the major religions. Some of the greatest violence has been among Christian denominations and between Muslim sects. An absolutist belief that a particular creed or movement within a religion is the truest, and therefore the greatest, has almost always eroded the multireligious drive to love God and neighbor.

Fortunately for me, my interfaith experiences have been better than Pi's. Whether from my childhood or through a University Religious Center or the South Coast Interfaith Council, I have experienced people being purposeful about coming together in mutual respect to find common ground, not to throw stereotypes at each other, but to listen and learn, to have our eyes opened, to respect one another as equals.

Hierarchies of Prejudice

It is always an effort to remain intentional; much of the time we remain subject to the lowest common denominator of perceptions. Our stereotypes and prejudices infiltrate quickly through our unconscious, even before we know what is happening, and we form hierarchies of prejudice in our hearts—and communities.

In John Sayles' movie *Lone Star*,[7] two middle-aged military men, both Anglos, talk to each other as one is about to marry an African-American woman.

His friend asks how her family feels about him being white.

He answers that she's in her late thirties, and they're just glad she isn't a lesbian.

The friend observes that there's nothing like overcoming one prejudice with a deeper prejudice.

In each person's heart—and in every congregation, school, corporation, organization, and institutional structure—there are layers, a hierarchy, of discrimination according to race, gender, class, religion, and sexual orientation. When a lesbian of color is discriminated against, it can be hard to know if it is because of her sexual orientation, gender, race, or the combination of all three.

In my experiences in two particular communities of faith that intentionally practiced diversity, each had different hierarchies of prejudice. At Holy Faith, there had been twenty years of work on racial integration before the congregation became bilingual and consciously multicultural. We started to address the issue of sexual orientation while I was there, but the level of stereotype and prejudice surrounding sexual orientation was far greater than around issues of race or culture, and we had only begun to address these deep-rooted concerns. We had done one kind of work far more than the other. At St. Luke's, the opposite was true: more and better work had been done on sexual orientation than on race and culture. The hierarchy of stereotype and prejudice in each person, each family, and each church is unique to its own history.

An old friend and mentor of mine, a white male, used to say that when he met with our African-American Suffragan Bishop, he didn't see him as black. I *suppose* what he was trying to say was that he didn't experience any gut-level feelings of prejudice against the bishop. In their relationship, they were two *people*. He spoke with great relief that he had outgrown a childhood prejudice, as if he were saying, "But now I see."

What he described, however, is what some call being "color blind." As one moves from blindness to sight, it *is* a step forward, but a small one. It replaces a blinding instinct with a new counter-instinct, a benign blindness in which we erase the stereotypical images that prevent us from seeing.

But instead of seeing *new* images, we see *no* images. If my friend did not see our bishop's race, then he did not see our bishop.

I know that for some this is a step in the right direction away from negative stereotypes and prejudices, but I had to ask my friend as gently as I could, "How do you not notice the color of someone's skin? Do you notice if someone is a woman or a man, an adult or a child, tall or short? If you hear someone, do you not notice if the person has an accent? Not reacting negatively is not the same thing as not noticing."

I often think of the process of moving away from our blinding instincts through the counter-instincts and beyond as parallel to the story of the healing of the blind man at Bethsaida (Mk 8:22–26). When Jesus spit on his hands and put saliva on the blind man's eyes, the blind man said that he could see people, but they looked like walking trees. He was seeing better perhaps, but he wasn't healed. Then Jesus put his hands on the man's eyes again. This time the man was completely healed; he saw clearly. While being "color blind" is better than being blinded by color or captured in one's prejudices, it is only one stage—and not a necessary one—in healing.

In the Buddhist tradition it is said that as you develop in the practice of meditation, first you see the mountain, and then you don't see it, and then you see it again.[8] First you see it superficially and then, because you are looking more deeply or too deeply at everything, you may miss it entirely. Finally, you see the mountain in all of its ordinary and extraordinary mountain-ness.

The same is true when our stereotypes and prejudices fall from our eyes like scales. If we are white or Asian or Latino, we may first see an African American *only* as a black person. Then, if we go through the stage of color-blindness, we may see an African American only as a person. We are completely healed only when we can see an African American as a person *and* a black person, as someone who shares the basics of humanity with persons of different racial backgrounds *and* as someone whose experience is partly shaped by the uniqueness of racial realities in our country. We may first see a Hindu through all of our stereotypes before we can see a human being who is also a Hindu, like us, and also different from us because of his/her beliefs. We may first see a lesbian only as gay, then as only human, and finally as gay and human. Or we may first see disabled persons as physically challenged before we can see them as fully human.

In our hierarchy of stereotypes and prejudices, each of us, like our sub-cultures and communities, develop unevenly and jaggedly. Personally, it was only in my thirties that I was forced to face my discomfort with persons who are physically challenged, something that other people face and overcome much earlier in life. When I was the Episcopal Chaplain at the University of California Santa Barbara, I met Phil, an Episcopalian who had cerebral palsy. While Phil had a serious side and was often very wise, he also had a hilarious sense of humor. When we walked through campus together—me walking, Phil riding in his motorized wheelchair—he loved to cut me off or bump me and pretend that I had hurt him. At first, I would self-consciously excuse myself, until he started laughing. He knew many people were uncomfortable with his physical condition, and he sometimes played along in mock healings to throw people off and, ultimately, to help people to see that he believed that God created him as he was and that he did not need to be "healed."

The goal of diversity is not color-blindness—or sexual orientation-blindness, or religion-blindness—although it is important that our inner eyes be healed of their prejudgments. The true goal is a *three-dimensional way of seeing* that takes into consideration our stereotypes and prejudices, each person's uniqueness, and our shared universal qualities.

Blinded to and by Systems

Overcoming the blindness caused by stereotypes and prejudices in the interpersonal realm is only one part of preparing ourselves for racial, religious, or cultural pluralism. In the twenty-third chapter of Matthew, the cogent criticisms Jesus had of the Pharisees are very applicable in the spiritual journey of diversity today: "Woe to you . . . for you tithe mint, dill, and cumin, and have neglected the weightier matters of the law: justice and mercy and faith. . . . You blind guides! You strain out a gnat but swallow a camel" (Mt 23:23–24).

While it is important that we rid ourselves of homophobia, racial prejudice, and religious self-righteousness on an interpersonal level, this is a little like straining out Jesus' proverbial gnat. If we don't address injustice on a systemic level, we've swallowed the whole camel! If we compare how many people we are going to injure with our personal prejudices—and how deeply we are going to hurt them—to how many more people will be crippled by the systems of misogyny, racism, homophobia, and classism, the larger scope of the problem becomes clear.

There is a simple racism test that I offer to those who are blind to systemic issues beyond the interpersonal level; those, for instance, who do not understand racism as prejudice plus power. Take any statistic about the racial breakdown of today's prison population, or the percentage of people—according to race—who are CEOs of our largest corporations or who graduate from high school. Look up the statistics! All of them show a disproportionate number of white people in positions of power, of people of color (especially Latinos and African Americans) dropping out of high school and entering prison instead of college or the work force. The same can be said of women's roles in society: How much less are women paid for doing the same jobs as men? Except in the public sector, it is *not* equal pay for equal work. More women than men live below the poverty line. More women than men are objects of violence.

One of the amazing things about social structures is that they still function even when they no longer have a practical social function, often even when they are counter-intuitive. Think how much more it must have cost to have separate bathrooms in the segregated South than to have one bathroom for each gender. It definitely cost more in apartheid-driven South Africa to transport Africans long distances by bus to their domestic cleaning jobs in white homes than if they lived nearby. But both ideologies dictated social policies that made no practical sense.

It also made no sense to build camps for Japanese Americans to live (and sometimes die) in during World War II when no such camps existed for German or Italian Americans; even then it would not have made much sense. It made even less sense to force Japanese Americans in those camps to say the pledge of allegiance each morning to the country that had stolen their property and treated them as criminals.[9] Likewise, the government, without conscious irony, used to force Native Americans living on reservations to sign a loyalty oath "without reservation."[10] Similarly, it makes no sense today that our national investment in public education from pre-school through higher education has diminished when there is a clear public benefit from a highly educated society.

From a Christian standpoint, this is when we recognize that the powers of evil are multidimensional. In baptism in the Episcopal Church, we "renounce Satan and all the spiritual forces of wickedness that rebel against God," "the evil powers of this world which corrupt and destroy the creatures of God," and "all sinful desires that draw you from the love of God." In other words, evil is cosmic and social, as well as personal. Most American religious traditions have focused almost exclusively on the personal dimension. In terms of the most damaging forms of evil in our society, however, to focus on personal sin and ignore social and cosmic evil is to strain out gnats and swallow camels.

William Stringfellow wrote convincingly about the social dimensions of evil, not only segregation and apartheid, but also nationalism, consumerism—even the church's craving to grow, grow, grow, as if growth were salvation. To him, every institution, every ideology, every public image of a person is a principality, in the biblical sense of "principalities and powers" (Eph 6:12),[11] concerned solely for its own preservation and power. To Stringfellow, this meant that every system, institution, and ideology automatically does its own sifting and sorting; that racism, sexism, homophobia, and religious zealotry are all spiritual entities concerned only with gaining and exerting more power. When we take part in these systems, when we give them our allegiance, we make ourselves their slaves.

The church, Stringfellow believed, is also a principality. When denominations fight, when there is an interreligious dispute—when the Episcopal Church wants more influence than the religious right, when Christians want more power in the world than Muslims—it is one principality vying with another for superiority. According to Stringfellow, to be blind to this, to believe that the Christian faith has only personal and interpersonal dimensions, is heretical.[12]

At a Clergy Conference in Los Angeles on race, I recall a senior priest—a white male who ran a large religious organization with a racially diverse staff—saying, "There is no such thing as white male domination in our society."

I tried not to laugh. Had he looked at who was in charge of his racially diverse organization? When I shared this comment with one of my brothers, he said, "Has he ever seen pictures of American presidents?"

In other words, the truth is right before our eyes all the time, but our "inner eyes," as Ellison called them, blind us to the truth because they make us see something that isn't there. Many, like this priest, prefer to focus on interpersonal prejudice instead of systemic discrimination. They chase gnats while swallowing camels. The religious right still asserts that the U.S. is or ought to be a Christian country, disdaining the atheists, agnostics, Jews, Muslims, Hindus, Buddhists, and practitioners of traditional Native American religion who are, or ought to be, equal citizens. They seek to force camels down the throats of those they disdain.

Social Dimensions of Blindness

I often compare people of the dominant culture, class, gender, and religion—people like myself—to Doubting Thomas. In the story of the Upper Room (Jn 20:19–29), Thomas refused to believe that Jesus had been raised from the dead. He said he had to see with his own eyes, to touch Jesus' wounds, before he would believe. Of course, when he did see Jesus and Jesus invited him to touch the wounds, Thomas' confession of faith exceeded any that had preceded it in John's Gospel. At the end of the story, however, Jesus pronounced a blessing on those who had not seen and yet believed.

But we come off much worse than Thomas because we go far beyond doubt. Even when we see the wounds of women, the poor, persons of color, gays and lesbians, and persons of other faiths, we still don't believe that they have been wounded. We *have* seen; we are sometimes even invited by courageous people to touch those wounds, and still we do not believe. We still insist that the system, whichever system it is, is impartial, fair, or—if flawed—capable of being reformed or simply the best we can do. Our childhood beliefs tell us so. Our inner eyes insist.

People of the dominant culture can also be very much like Job's so-called friends. When a woman or a poor person or a gay person or a person of color or a Muslim or a Jew tells us stories of suffering or discrimination, we—as spokespersons for the system—say or imply, "It must be your fault. You must have done something wrong. It must be your family's fault. They must have made self-destructive decisions." In other words, we become pharisaical judges of others, and thus put ourselves under God's judgment.

Abraham Lincoln was much more sophisticated in his understanding of evil and judgment in a time of polarization and horrific violence. He came to understand the Civil War as God's judgment on a nation that practiced slavery. It was not merely a judgment on the South; it was also a judgment on the complicity of the North, which profited from slavery even though it did not take a direct role in it, even though it pushed—half- or wholeheartedly—for its abolition.

Gandhi had a similar intuition about India under the British Raj. India, he said, could not be free until the *dalits* (Untouchables) were treated as equals.[13] If India gained its political independence and still practiced injustice, that was not freedom. It was merely an extension of an oppressive system under indigenous rulers, the old oppressions under new management. From this viewpoint, then, the results of the American Revolution are yet to be determined: Is there really freedom or "liberty and justice for all"? Until there is justice for all, the nation is not free.

There have been steps toward justice—suffrage for men of color, later suffrage for women, the end of legalized discrimination against persons of color—but there have also been steps sideways and backward. The church, likewise, as an organization, can *say* it is following Jesus, but it isn't following very closely or carefully until it treats all people equally at the altar when they seek communion, or ordination, or a blessing on their committed relationship.

When I was at Holy Faith, I was sometimes struck by the images that some African and African-American parishioners had of each other. More than once, I heard a Nigerian parishioner say that, while they knew a few who were dif-ferent, African Americans tended to be poor, uneducated, and violent. More than once, I heard an African-American parishioner say that, while they knew one or two who were different, most Africans tended to be poor, uneducated, and violent. More than once, I asked them where they got these images. The answer was from the white-dominated media that perpetuated racist stereotypes by what it showed on local and national news.

Yet even to attribute an intentionality to promote racism to the producers of the newscasts would miss the point. It is built into the principality of the media; the media is on auto-pilot to show images that reinforce stereotypes, prejudice, racism, and discrimination. It takes a conscious effort by those who have a three-dimensional view of race—*and* by those who have clarity about the power of institutions, ideologies, and images—to counter our ingrained and institutionally rewarded habits.

To heal the social dimension of our blindness, we need to understand the *other* as well as we know ourselves. If we do not know the other, we cannot begin to respect the con-tents of their "well," the ways their lives—their "cells"—have been shaped, the ways they have known or questioned God. When we meet someone different from ourselves in any way, we are connecting with a person formed—as we are partially formed—by the systems and sub-cultures and the society in which they have lived.

When I was growing up in Los Angeles in the fifties, it was as homophobic an environment as any I can imagine. It was only by hearing the experiences of gay and lesbian friends and reflecting on my faith that I began to cope with and rein in my own stereotypes and prejudices. Most of the progress in our church—and our society—on issues of sexual orientation is due to gay and lesbian persons who have had the courage to let their families, friends, and neighbors know who they are. When we open ourselves to the experience of the person in the next pew, when we acquire new information, we can begin to dismantle heterosexist prejudgments and overcome our stereotypes.

Yet when it comes to any stereotype or prejudice, none of us are ever completely healed or free. As much as we can be healed, all people suffer from internalized racism and sexism and homophobia. The inner eyes, while partially corrected, are never entirely healed.

This was subtly evident when our church in the Santa Barbara area bought a small house in the eighties. We moved it to our property so that we could open a homeless shelter as part of a faith-based organization called Transition House. Transition House was born from the work of congregations banding together to respond to the then-new phenomenon of massive homelessness. Our goal was to work with those who were willing and able to get a job, to help them find housing and sustain themselves. Transition House took pride in being different from shelters where homeless persons who wanted to spend the night were required to hear a sermon and/or to confess their faith before receiving a bed. Transition House felt uncomfortable with proselytizing that took advantage of people's economic vulnerability. Jesus did not preach to people before he healed them; he did not suggest that the Samaritan have the man in the ditch sign an oath before he helped him (Lk 10:30–35). Transition House, however, did expect homeless persons who took part in the program to share middle-class values before we were willing to help. Unless someone wanted a place to live and a forty-hour-a-week job, they were turned away. In other words, we, too, had our biases but, because they were class biases instead of overtly theological ones, they were invisible to us.

Our biases never seem as destructive as the biases of others. We see clearly how *others* are like Doubting Thomas, how *others* are like Job's friends, how *others* strain gnats and swallow camels. The social dimensions of blindness are especially difficult to overcome because we are immersed in the shared illusions of our churches, culture, and class. We are tempted to see what we are told to see. It is only through a transformation of the "eyes of our heart" (Eph 1:18) that we can be healed.

Spiritual Dimensions of Blindness

Just as there is a social dimension to our blindness about class and race, so there is a spiritual dimension.

When I helped to design a White Racial Awareness Process in the mid-nineties with the National Conference for Community and Justice, I was never disappointed by white people's ability to feel either defensive or guilty about racism. The point, of course, is to get past defensiveness and guilt, to take *responsibility* for the reality of racism—and our part in it—and to use whatever power we have to actively work against racism in all of its dimensions. Against those powers of racism, our idealism and our ideology are externals. Jesus said that the Pharisees liked to clean the outside of the cup while the inside was filled with greed (Mt 23:25–26). In other words, our introspection needs to go deeper than idealism and ideology. Those are on the outside of the cup. We need to look within, with eyes wide open, at what comes out of our own hearts.

I think of again Tagore's statement that the U.S. today would not allow Jesus to enter the country because he was poor and belonged to the wrong race. This raises questions that we each must face: *Why do we allow this to be true? Do we let the real Jesus into our hearts, or do we substitute a middle-class, Anglo savior for the first-century Palestinian Jew that Jesus really was?*

During Holy Week in 2003, after the U.S. had invaded Iraq, it struck me harshly that to be a dark-skinned religious fanatic was no more valued by our society than it was by the Roman Empire that crucified Jesus. It is still dangerous. We have replaced the Roman Empire as the power in the world that has no use for those we see and define as dark-skinned religious fanatics.

Yet often people like myself—from the dominant culture—overestimate our power. Martin Luther King, Jr. said that the doors that separate the oppressors from the oppressed are locked from both sides.[14] This is true with every form of difference—race, gender, sexual orientation, class, and religion. If the doors between people are to be unlocked, then there must be people on both sides to open them. In the Civil Rights movement, the white power structure had the power to undo injustice; but the African-American community had the spiritual power—the greater power—to forgive and redeem and make reconciliation possible.

In any relationship out-of-balance because of differences in power, this dynamic tends to be in place. The physical power lies where we would expect it to be, but the spiritual power always belongs to the marginalized. Those who profit most from the power structure have the most to gain spiritually from reconciliation. Jesus spoke words that would benefit most Americans who seem literally hell-bent on acquiring material things, words that would benefit the U.S. as our nation seems equally hell-bent to acquire more and more power: "What will it profit them to gain the whole world and forfeit their life?" (Mk 8:36).

One of the themes in Thomas Merton's writings is blindness and sight. In his preface to the writings of the Desert Christians, he said that their goal of leaving cities for the desert was to gain a clear and unobstructed view of the world as it really was. In his introduction to the writings of Gandhi, Merton described a "one-eyed giant" (the West) that was blinded by its view of itself as an all-good, all-seeing force. During the war in Vietnam, Merton described American foreign policy as a continuation of the nineteenth-century historical pattern and twentieth-century game of cowboys and Indians.

There is plenty of blindness to go around in any generation, and we would like to think that none of it is our fault. There are wars; there is racism; there is poverty; there is discrimination against people for any, every, and no reason; there are systems in place to assure that there will be discrimination. Merton said that the fact that he was born during World War I or that he was a contemporary of the Holocaust and the war in Vietnam and race riots was not something about which he was consulted beforehand. But, like it or not, he was deeply involved and implicated in those terrible realities of his time.[15]

The problem for contemporary American Christians, Merton wrote, is similar to that of the fourth-century Christians who fled to the desert: how to take a step outside the culture in order to gain a clear unpolluted view of current events.

Merton prescribed prayer. Prayer, he said, "transforms our vision of the world, and makes us see it . . . in the light of God."[16] Like Stringfellow, Merton knew that Americans see life "Americanly," from the top floor of towers—whether they occupy those offices or identify with those who do. Merton's prescription for our spiritual blindness is to see life contemplatively, from the experience of God in prayer.

Sight for the Blind

As we seek our own healing, it is important to recall that there is almost always a subtext in the Gospel's healing stories. In John's Gospel, there are seven stories about Jesus' ministry that are followed by explanatory dialogues and monologues. One of these is a complicated and ironic story in the ninth chapter of John. It is the only story in which Jesus temporarily disappeared from center stage while the other characters worked through layers of irony in a story of healing and blindness.

First, there was the man who was born blind, but it was the disciples who revealed their spiritual blindness when they asked Jesus if the man was blind because of his own sin or because of the sin of his parents. They took the "Job's comforters" approach to suffering: If you suffer, it must be your own fault. In addition to your own suffering, you have to bear the weight of projected responsibility for your suffering! (This is similar to what Dorothy Day described as the burden of the poor in America: to bear scorn and blame on top of the already terrible burden of poverty.[17])

Jesus responded to his disciples, saying that neither the man nor his parents were the cause. Instead, he told his disciples to think of the man's blindness as an opportunity for God's work to be done and, specifically in this instance, for Jesus to show that he was the light of the world. Jesus spit on the dirt to make mud, spread the mud on the man's eyes, and told him to wash his eyes. When the man washed, he saw.

It was then that the blindness of his neighbors was revealed, for they had only seen the man—categorized and stereotyped him—as a blind beggar, a one-dimensional human being entirely different from themselves, physically challenged, and poor. They had not seen him as a person; they had only seen him as blind and a beggar. They started to argue with each other about whether this healed person was the same as the one who had been blind: How could he be the same man if he could now see? The only thing that identified him was his blindness!

The neighbors then took the man to the Pharisees, who began the inquiry all over again: How could he see? The man rehearsed the details. But the Pharisees objected because, in their view, Jesus could not be "from God" because he did not strictly observe the Sabbath; he did not share their interpretation of the faith.

The Pharisees, like the neighbors, found themselves divided. Some believed their physical eyes: the man was blind and now he could see. How could this happen unless the healing was "from God"? So they asked the man-formerly-known-as-the-blind-man what he thought of Jesus. He replied, "He is a prophet." In John's view, this was an answer that saw only part of the truth, as if the mud didn't quite work the first time. But the healing went on as the man continued to be confronted by the spiritually blind.

Still not satisfied, the religious authorities called in the man's parents to hear what they would say: "Is this your son who was born blind? How can he see?"

They answered in the affirmative, saying that their son had been born blind, but they didn't know how it was that he could see or who had healed him. "Ask *him*," they retorted.

For the second time, the Pharisees summoned the man. When they told him that Jesus was a sinner, the man answered that he didn't know about that. He knew only that he had been blind but could now see. He chose the visible evidence over the opinion of the religious leaders. Not satisfied, they asked him to repeat his story. At this point, either eager or sarcastic, he asked them, "Why? Do you want to become his disciples?" This enraged them, and they accused the man of secretly being one of Jesus' disciples, maybe even implying that he was a shill.

The man, working his way into a more profound faith, argued inductively from his own experience. Jesus had opened his eyes. Clearly, God had done this, since who else could heal the blind? Clearly, then, Jesus was from God. Ultimately, the religious leaders drove him away.

Jesus found the man again and asked if he believed in the Son of Man. The man answered, "Lord I believe," and he worshipped Jesus. Then Jesus put a punctuation mark on the end of the story, saying that he came into the world "so that those who do not see may see, and those who do see may become blind" (Jn 9:39).

When we can get past our defensiveness and be honest with ourselves about our blindness, we have a choice: We can receive our blindness as either good or bad news, as a judgment that we cannot evade or as a diagnosis that can be healed.

There is a story from the Hindu tradition about Lord Shiva coming down from his holy abode on Mount Kailasha and disguising himself as a saint, while his wife, Parvati, disguised herself as his disciple. They came to the world to give people salvation and entered a town where they sat in a secluded place. If anyone came to the saint (Shiva in disguise), Shiva told the person his past and future. As often happened in the Gospels when people heard that Jesus had entered a village, flocks of people came to meet this saint.

One pilgrim, who appeared to be the leader of a group, came forward, bowed to the saint, and asked humbly, "Will you tell me when I will get salvation?" The pilgrim proceeded to tell the saint how much he had meditated during the winter and during the summer, how modest his diet was: for several years, he had only eaten a daily meal of fruit and milk.

The saint looked at him and said, "You are a very good yogi. You have much devotion."

Hearing this, the man felt excited that he would hear about his salvation. The saint continued: "At this rate you can get salvation after three births [reincarnations]." The pilgrim was shocked, mumbled to his group, and sighed despondently "still three births." He had thought he was closer to salvation.

Others came forward. Another told the saint about his *sadhana* (spiritual practice); the saint listened and said it would take him seven births to find salvation. Another would take ten births, another fifteen, others twenty or thirty. Finally, when all the others were finished, a small, thin, ugly man who had been hiding behind the others came forward. He was shy and afraid. He told the saint, "I don't do any *sadhana*, but I love God's creation, and I try not to hurt anyone by my actions, thoughts, or words. Can I get salvation?"

The saint scratched his head as if he were in doubt. The man bowed again and nervously repeated his question.

The saint finally replied, "If you go on loving God in the same way, maybe after a thousand births you, too, will get salvation"

As soon as he heard it the man was ecstatic and began to dance and shout: "I can get salvation! I can get salvation!" As he continued to shout, all of a sudden his body changed into flame. At the same time the saint (Shiva) and his disciple (Parvati) also changed into flame. All three flames merged into one and disappeared.

When they returned to their abode at Mount Kailasha, Parvati confessed to Shiva that she was confused. "You told the leader that he would need three births, but when you told the ugly man that he would get salvation in a thousand births, you gave it to him instantly."

Shiva replied that, though the leader had a strong *sadhana*, his egotism slowed his journey toward salvation. His egotism made three births seem a long time. The ugly, thin man, however, had so much faith that even a thousand births seemed very short for him. Shiva said, "He completely surrendered to me. I did not give him salvation; it was his own faith in my words."[18]

This Hindu story has resonances with several Gospel stories. Jesus told the rich young man—who had done so many things right—that there was one more thing he needed to do, and the man went away disappointed (Mk 10:17–22). Zacchaeus, on the other hand, was like the small, thin, ugly man who, when he realized that he had even a *chance* for salvation, found his life set ablaze by this revelation.

In one of Jesus' parables, a Pharisee said, "God, I thank you that I am not like other people." Like the egotistical pilgrim, he had been justly proud of his spiritual practices, while a tax collector, who had also come to the temple to pray, had nothing but his humility. Again, it was the penitent who accurately assessed his life who went home in right relationship with God (Lk 18:9–13).

It is not the assessment about how far we have to go or

how much blindness we have to overcome that matters; it is the way we receive the news, the diagnosis of our condition, that counts. Those who believe they have traveled a long way toward perfection are those who will be most disappointed. Those who are glad that they still have a chance may find themselves, because of their joyful relief, much closer to their goal than they had imagined.

Spiritual Exercise: My Images

This spiritual exercise requires privacy and honesty. Fill it out as if you never have to share any of it with anyone except God.

Start by choosing one *race/ethnic group/culture*: Anglo, Latino, African American, Arab, Korean, Vietnamese, Native American, etc. (The more courageous you feel, the more you will be inclined to consider a group with which you have the most difficulty.) In each quadrant, write down what you learned about this group from your family of origin, from your religious upbringing, from the media, and from your own personal experience.

Then choose one *religion or religious group*—Roman Catholic, Muslim, Buddhist, Jew, Sikh, Hindu, or fundamentalist Christian—and again write in each quadrant what you learned from each of the four aspects of your experience.

Do this a third time with a *sexual orientation or gender.*

Conclude by choosing a *social class*—probably the one with which you are least familiar and/or have the most stereotypes—and complete the four quadrants.

Take some time to reflect on what you have written. What positive and/or negative stereotypes do you have of various groups? Consider what might help you move beyond your instinctive stereotypes to see people of these groups in a humanized, *three-dimensional* way. Would it help to learn more about this group? Would it help to meet a person from this group?

MY IMAGES

FAMILY	RELIGIOUS UPBRINGING
Race/Ethnic Group/Culture: Religion: Sexual Orientation/Gender: Social Class:	Race/Ethnic Group/Culture: Religion: Sexual Orientation/Gender: Social Class:
Race/Ethnic Group/Culture: Religion: Sexual Orientation/Gender: Social Class:	Race/Ethnic Group/Culture: Religion: Sexual Orientation/Gender: Social Class:
MEDIA	**PERSONAL EXPERIENCE**

Spiritual Counsel

Meditate on one of the following quotations each day during the next week. As you do so, ask yourself these questions:

- How does this touch my heart?
- How does it affect the way I wish to interact with people I meet, especially people of a different gender, sexual orientation, religion, or race?
- How does it help me see large groups of people, especially people of other nations, cultures, races, and religions?

"Then Jesus laid his hands on his eyes again; and he looked intently and his sight was restored, and he saw everything clearly."—Mark 8:25

"Dissolve your whole body into Vision. Become seeing, seeing, seeing!"—Rumi

"You must be nothing but an ear which hears what the universe of the word is constantly saying within you."—Dov Baer of Mezritch

"When I was a child, I spoke like a child, I thought like a child, I reasoned like a child, but when I became an adult, I put an end to childish ways."—1 Corinthians 13:11

"You strain out a gnat, but swallow a camel!"—Matthew 23:24

Spiritual Practice

- After meditating on one of the Spiritual Counsel quotations, do a mental census of the diversity in your area, town, suburb, neighborhood, or city. Include race, religion, class, and sexual orientation. Then compare your mental census with actual figures from recent census data. (This data is easily accessible on the Internet.)

- Talk with another family member—preferably from your generation—about the stereotypes and prejudices that your family of origin encouraged. Find out what that family member has done to overcome those stereotypes and prejudices.

CHAPTER 4
Becoming Bread

A peasant goes to town and, for the first time, enters a bakery. It is as if he has entered paradise. In the bakery, the scent of breads, pastries, and cakes swarms his senses. He savors the smell, and as he tastes each bite, he is rapt with delight.

In awe, he asks the baker, "How do you make the bread? How do you make the cakes?"

The baker shows him his ovens.

Looking at the dough, the peasant asks, "Where does this come from?"

The baker replies, "From wheat."

As if returning to earth, the peasant says with a mix of discovery and satisfaction, "I have wheat. I have kernels and shafts. I have everything that you have. What I have is the same as bread."

His senses satisfied and his mind at ease with a dull-witted conclusion, he leaves the bakery convinced that the baker has nothing he doesn't have.

He equates the raw materials of bread with bread itself.[1]

This story from the Jewish tradition describes the person who has all the raw materials but has not integrated them into a whole. Having the raw materials is not enough. In order to *become* bread, to be a source of life and sustenance to others, we need to refine what we have been given. If we want to make diversity part of our normal spiritual practice, we need to take our unrefined thoughts, intuitions, and hopes and turn them into bread.

The raw materials of diversity start with the self-awareness of our "cell," which is nurtured by an awareness of our religious tradition, and through it, of God, and is deepened by our understanding of other peoples. These are the "wheat" from which we can bake loaves and cakes. Jesus said, "I am the bread of life"; as members of Christ's body, *we* are that bread.

But what if our "raw materials" do not include opportunities for cross-cultural or interfaith relationships in our daily lives? While creating the White Racial Awareness Process in the mid-1990s, one of our foundational principles was that if white people can learn racism without the presence of people of color, we can unlearn racism without relying on the presence of people of color.

For those stuck in homogeneous or isolated lives, Thomas Merton is a good role model. Decades ago, he said that one of the critical spiritual tasks of our age is to find something in common with persons from cultures completely different from our own.[2] From the geographical seclusion of his Kentucky hermitage, Merton managed—well before the Internet—to reach out and embrace people of entirely divergent backgrounds. His example is a lesson and a model for those who live apart from diversity—whether it is a rural environment, suburban ghettoization, or an island in an archipelago of homogeneity. Merton corresponded with persons of many religious, racial, and ethnic backgrounds, always in a spirit of reciprocity and mutual respect. Given the technological advances in communications over the past fifty years, the possibilities for us are immeasurable.

Yet even if we are blessed with the most propitious circumstances, and many forms of diversity are part of our every day existence, it is not an easy thing to sustain our awareness. We hinder ourselves constantly by our limited sight, imagination, and commitment.

In the Old Testament story of Elijah's battle with the priests of Baal, Elijah confronted the Israelites with a pointed question: "How long will you go limping between two opinions?" (1 Kings 18:21). The question is an apt one for us: How long will we limp along between our values and wants, and our presumed needs? How long will we try to combine two ways of life into one? How long will we commit ourselves to two kinds of gods? It is akin to Jesus' statement that we cannot serve God and wealth (Mt 6:24). As long as we cling to two ways of thinking, two ways of believing, two ways of living, there is no way for us to run the race, as Paul says (1 Cor 9:24–26, Gal 2:2, Phil 2:16); we will only move at a slow, feeble limp.

It is a commonplace in many religious traditions to speak of life as a path. In the tenth century, Symeon the New Theologian described a road not only with gardens, peopled by saints, but also with beasts and thieves.[3] Life is a complicated thoroughfare, alternately and sometimes simultaneously perilous and wondrous. The mystical path in classical Christian writing has three stages that offer us some help on the long road to diversity: purgation, illumination, and union.

Purgation

In the first step, *purgation*, we are stripped of all the things that get in the way of our relationship with God and neighbor. This can include external property and habits, giving things up for Lent being a classic example. This step also includes dispensing with pride, self-righteousness, security, paternalism, and judgmentalism. It can mean letting go of our privileges. It can also mean curing the wounds that others have inflicted on us. When we put aside the things that "corrupt and destroy the creatures of God"—greed, lust, malice, slander, dishonesty (Col 3:6–10)—then we can "clothe" ourselves with compassion, kindness, meekness, humility, and patience (v. 12). Purgation clears the way for a new relationship with God and neighbor.

Soren Kierkegaard observed that the people in the greatest despair are those who do not know they are in despair. The people who need the most stringent spiritual discipline and practice are often those who do not think they need them at all. The people with the greatest need for purgation are often the ones who find it hardest to embark on that path.

Several religious traditions agree that it is best to correct the meek gently and rebuke the recalcitrant strongly. Some people are too easily chastised and ready to confess (or glory) in guilt. Others are very slow to awaken because they have lulled themselves into complacency. Either way, it is hard to purge ourselves of the things that keep us from becoming bread for the sake of others. It is hard to truly believe that circumcision and uncircumcision are meaningless; that our gender, ethnic identity, religious affiliation, and cultural values are insignificant compared to our adherence to God.

Jesus advised those around him to first remove the log from their own eye before trying to remove the speck from the eye of their neighbor (Mt 7:3–5). That is terrific guidance for us: not to seek out every tiny flaw in the practice of another religious tradition, but to use our energy to reform ourselves and our faith community. It is wise guidance to people of any race or culture—but especially those of the dominant culture—to be cautious about criticizing others. It is particularly helpful to Christians to remove the obstacles from our eyes before we stereotype Jews or Muslims or Hindus in a particular way.

When we began conversations at St. Luke's about starting a service in Spanish, one lay leader expressed a "concern" that Latinos might not have our tradition of stewardship and might not be a self-supporting part of the church. Since St. Luke's had been in existence for over a hundred years and still did not have a strong tradition of stewardship among English-speakers and, in fact, needed income from its endowment and its property to balance its budget, there wasn't much to say. Talk about needing to first remove the log from one's own eye!

The clarity of purgation doesn't come easily, and it requires that we ask some soul-searching questions. If we want to purge ourselves of unhealthy attitudes toward others, we need to consider who "they" are. Who are the people at the fringes of our experience at church, at work, and in our families? Who are the people at the center of our relationships? Are they homogeneous? How are they heterogeneous? Who are the people we do not respect, people who—in our private moments—we might put down, directly or indirectly? Whom do we "tolerate?" Who are the people—the "they," whomever "they" are—that make us uncomfortable? Whose opinions do we dismiss without even considering the content of their thoughts? Instead of pointing to the speck in their eyes, what would it mean for us to remove the log from our own eyes so that we could see them differently?

Illumination

As we make the transition from purgation and turn toward the second step, *illumination*, we are taking the good raw materials that are within us and turning them into bread. As we do this, we would do well to recall a memorable phrase from the First Epistle of John: "Perfect love casts out fear" (1 John 4:18).

These words sound like a cosmic battle in which we may

feel ill-equipped. Yet we need to follow up John's profound statement with two questions. Who is perfect? No one. Whose fear is perfect? No one's. Imperfect love battles our imperfect fear. We are not expected to be perfect, but we are expected to move toward compassion, holiness, and love. What frightens us? *Who* scares us? How can we love them in such a way that it eases fear's grip on our lives? How can we love them so that we will turn toward them instead of acting defensively to protect our cowering hearts?

Illumination is spiritual enlightenment that comes through revelations, large and small. It is a period of listening and looking and learning from God. In the Christian year, it is most closely associated with Epiphany, the season of light in which we discover "the knowledge of the glory of God in the face of Jesus Christ" (2 Cor 4:6). It is an ongoing experience of discipleship. Part of that experience is discovering the face of Christ in every human face.

As the conflagration died down after the 1992 Los Angeles riot/uprising, my assistant and I telephoned as many of our parishioners as we could to see if they had survived the violence unscathed, at least physically. Everyone had a story to tell: keeping their young children indoors, lying flat on their floors as they heard gunshots outside their homes, inhaling smoke from nearby fires, and an eerie sense of calm after the chaos. The church itself was virtually abandoned for two days. When I told one parishioner I was going to return to the office the next morning, she said, "Be careful. You aren't the right color just now."

The revelation in her words was twofold, of course. For the briefest of times, it was dangerous, a disadvantage, to be white, and she wanted to remind me, as if I needed reminding. It was everywhere obvious that it was unsafe to be *any-body* for those few days. Perhaps she thought that I would be blinded by my skin color or even by an illusion that wearing a collar might give me some kind of ecclesiastical immunity. Churches, after all, had been respected for the most part;

only a few had been collateral damage from neighboring fires. But even more so, the words I remember are the "just now," a reminder that in most times and most places my skin color was the *right* color to be.

For days and weeks afterward, when people of different races passed each other on the streets, there was a need to acknowledge each other in a deeper way. There was very little looking past the person walking the other way on the street. It was a time of heightened sensitization; it was an awakening. The normal quick glances took longer. We studied each other's faces. We looked into each other's eyes for signs of sorrow and caring and hope, and Christ. In my experience, most of the time we found what we sought.

Union

Just as purgation prepares us for illumination, illumination, in turn, prepares us for *union* with God. This is the "communion" we experience at the altar during the Eucharist. This is to dwell in Christ and to know that Christ lives in us (Gal 2:20). This is to be one with God as Christ was one in God (Jn 17:11).

One of my favorite prayers speaks of "loving [God] in all things and above all things" (the Collect for the Sixth Sunday of Easter in the Book of Common Prayer). The prayer attests to a delicate spiritual balance and a simultaneous interpenetration. As the second phrase states, God is the one we are called to love more than we love anyone else or anything else in creation. Yet as the first phrase says, we love God by loving everyone and everything that God has made.

The early Christian writer Dorotheus of Gaza offered a brilliant way to visualize the progress we make in uniting with God and neighbor:

Suppose we were to take a compass and insert the point and draw the outline of a circle. The centre point

is the same distance from any point on the circumference. . . . Let us suppose that this circle is the world
and that God . . . is the centre; the straight lines drawn
from the circumference to the centre are the lives of
[people]. To the degree that the saints enter into the
things of the spirit, they desire to come near to God;
and in proportion to their progress in the things of the
spirit, they do in fact come close to God and to their
neighbor. The closer they are to God, the closer they
become to one another; and the closer they are to one
another, the closer they become to God. . . . If we were
to love God more, we should be closer to God, and
through love of [God] we should be more united in
love to our neighbor; and the more we are united to
our neighbor the more we are united to God.[4]

Dorotheus' visual image incorporates some of our faith's
most basic teachings about love. In 1 John, the mentor of the
community taught that whoever says, "I love God" but does
not love fellow members of the faith community is a liar
(4:20). The two great commandments to love God and neighbor (Mt 22:37–40) do not simply stand side-by-side; they in-
terpenetrate each other. Likewise, Jesus does not allow us to
be self-satisfied with loving family and friends and the familiar: "If you love those who love you, what credit is that to
you? For even sinners love those who love them. If you do
good to those who do good to you, what credit is that to you?
For even sinners do the same" (Lk 6:32–33).

If we are indeed drawing toward the center of the circle,
others can tell us if our awareness and our desire to love are
bearing fruit. There is a Buddhist saying that truth without
action is like flower without a scent.[5] As 1 John insists, we
must love "not in word or speech, but in truth and action"
(3:18).

A priest who served the Catholic Worker community as a

spiritual director taught that we love God only as much as the person we love least.[6] We love God only as much as we love the homeless person, the judgmental fundamentalist, the corrupt CEO of a bankrupted corporation, or the person of another political party, sexual orientation, race, or religion. In today's multifaith environment, Dorotheus' circle implies that as the Christian draws closer to God we also draw nearer to the Muslim, the Jew, the Sikh, the Buddhist, and the Hindu. If we are bread, others will notice that we smell like a fresh loaf. As we move toward union with God, we will move into greater unity with everyone God has created.

Becoming Allies

It is common to fall into delusions about our unity with others. Many people have said, "Some of my 'best friends' are black, gay, and/or Jewish," as if that meant that they were in sympathy with all African Americans, all persons in the gay/lesbian community, all Jews. If we want to become bread, we have to become more than friends with people on an interpersonal basis.

Two classic twentieth-century novels portray the difference between responding to an individual or to a community. In Albert Camus's novel *The Fall*, the protagonist, Jean-Baptiste Clamence, made this confession in a bar: Late one night, as he was going home from the Left Bank, he passed a young woman leaning over a railing. Moments later, he heard the sound of her body hitting the water. Then he heard her cry out several times as she was swept downstream. Finally, the cries stopped. He thought about doing something to save the woman, but in a split second, the chance passed, and he did nothing.[7]

Elie Wiesel recounts a different kind of story in *The Town Beyond the Wall*. Wiesel, himself a Holocaust survivor, tells the story of Michael, who had also survived a concentration camp and after the war retraced his steps to the village square where Nazis had rounded up Jews. As he revisited the square, Michael remembered his experience years before. He had looked up into an open window and seen the face of a man surveying the tragedy without even a crease of sorrow, compassion, fear, or remorse appearing on his face. Reflecting on that memory, Michael wrote, "The executioners I understood; also the victims, though with more difficulty. For the others, all the others, those who were neither for nor against, those who sprawled in passive patience . . . those who thought themselves above the battle, those who were permanently and merely spectators—all those were closed to me, incomprehensible."[8]

While Camus describes a failure to respond to a person in need, Wiesel portrays someone who is unwilling or unable to be an ally, someone with a stillborn reflex to care for, or even care about, a people in crisis.

To become bread means being an *ally* of others, whoever they are, realigning our values to make their well-being a top priority in our lives. But American culture is much more attuned to being a friend in need than it is to becoming an ally. The evening news becomes transfixed day after day with small, personal stories—trials of celebrities, murders of individuals—while virtually ignoring the major traumas of whole peoples: genocide in Cambodia, Bosnia, Rwanda, and Sudan. Poverty and oppression are norms for most of the world. Injustices are the daily bread of many people in our local communities. But the local news averts its eyes, staring at gnats while ignoring camels.

The more closely we are united with God, the more our awareness will become balanced, and the more often we will act on our awareness. The story is told of the thirteenth-century Sufi poet and mystic Rumi that one of his young disciples was alarmed one day when his teacher, supposedly an ascetic, asked him to bring his master a large dish of rich food. The suspicious disciple followed Rumi as he carried the food through the streets, into the fields and finally into the ruins of a tomb. There the disciple saw Rumi bending over to feed by hand an exhausted mother dog and her six puppies. In awe, the disciple, giving himself away, asked, "How did you know they were here? How did you know they were hungry?"

Rumi answered, "The one who is fully awake can hear the cry of a sparrow from ten thousand miles away."[9]

Here was an ally of every living creature responding specifically to a few. Here was someone who had drawn near to God and so had entered unto union with everything that God has made.

This feeding of the dogs might resonate with Christians who recall the story in which Jesus met the Syrophoenician woman and described Gentiles as "dogs" (Mk 7:24–30). In that story, we see the fallible side of Jesus and how many barriers must be surmounted in order for people to meet one another as children of God. Jesus initially treated the Gentile (*strike one*) woman (*strike two*) as an outcast. She called him by the exclusivist title "Son of David" (*strike three*). His ministry, his concern, was only to feed—to bring bread, to be bread—for the lost sheep of the house of Israel (*four strikes, as if three were not enough*). Should he, he asked her, take the children's bread and give it to the dogs (*how many strikes are needed*)? Her reply changed his mind: "Sir, even the dogs under the table eat the children's crumbs" (v. 28). In the end, she received more than crumbs. Jesus commended her faith—a woman's faith, a foreign faith— and he healed her daughter. Jesus became the ally of a dispossessed outcast.

Being an ally means making constant connections between our awareness of our selves (individually and collectively), God, and other peoples. When Muriel Lester walked among the dead bodies in the aftermath of a Shanghai battle, she was very aware of Europe's imperialistic domination. When she found pieces of shrapnel, she knew they had been made from scrap iron that Japan had imported from Britain and the United States. She knew that her own country's economic policies had strengthened Japan's militaristic imperialism. She saw how British and American economic interests, which had carved out "spheres of influence" in China, now worked hand-in-hand with Japanese aggression to take human lives, to expand new spheres of violence and suffering. She knew that her own country had been an accomplice in the deaths of these young men.[10] Lester could see the ways that the very nations that would soon be at war with Japan had profited from the wholesale slaughter. As she traveled through China, even as she directly confronted her Chinese audiences on the issue of opium use, she always bracketed her remarks by confessing British involvement in the drug trade.[11] Unlike Wiesel's "Other," Lester saw the connections, told the truth about what she saw, and protested against violence and injustice.

Being an ally means heeding Gandhi's advice to "recall the face of the poorest person you have seen, and ask yourself if the next step you take will be of any use to that person."[12] Being an ally means being a *zaddik*, a righteous person, one who is fully awake, responding to both the drowning person in the river and to the whole people feeling the shark's bite of persecution. The *zaddik* is always an activist, always an abolitionist, always an advocate for human rights, and always a seeker for the well-being of undocumented workers, a pursuer of universal health care, and safe and affordable housing for all of God's people.

Becoming an ally means taking the risks that Camus's Jean-Baptiste Clamence and Wiesel's "Other" did *not* take. Becoming an ally means stepping outside of our comfort zone.

For me, a particularly uncomfortable area in my life is

speaking in any language other than English. Starting in high school, I've tried to learn several—French, Hausa, Greek, Hebrew, and Spanish. Given my miserable linguistic skills, it was initially awkward being a priest in a bilingual parish (in fact, I do not recommend it except as a transitional strategy). While another priest developed the Spanish-speaking part of the congregation, I tried to learn to worship in Spanish phonetically so that I could at least *sound* all right as I sang and prayed. Even this took me hours of preparation. Yet the first time I had to celebrate the Eucharist in Spanish, I would have gladly traded it to dance naked in a bar (and I don't even like to dance). I felt *that* exposed. The experience was both humbling and humiliating. However, as poor a job as I did—and I did it often—I at least stepped out of my comfort zone. Whatever our comfort zone, being willing to expand it is a sign of a commitment to become an ally.

Understanding Our Motivations

Becoming an ally is one thing. Recognizing what motivates and drives one to be an ally is another. One of the exercises we used in the White Racial Awareness Process illustrates three possible spiritual motivations.[13] Some people approach diversity as way to implement the *Golden Rule*: Do to others as you would have others do to you (Lk 6:31). Diversity, from this point of view, primarily tries to discover each person's humanity and uncover the ways we are similar to one another. From this perspective, it is first and foremost a matter of individuals changing their attitudes and their behavior.

Others approach diversity as a matter of justice and seek to *right the wrong*. They recognize that some people have been systematically disadvantaged while others have been privileged. In this approach, diversity requires equality and justice to rectify imbalances in society.

The third perspective *values all differences*. This approach appreciates and respects the gifts of each culture and sub-culture, each religious tradition, and each collective experience. It assumes that when we engage in diversity, everyone is mutually enriched.

While these approaches are distinctly different from each other, they can be complementary. Whatever their distinctiveness, each one inspires the person seeking diversity to become an ally.

St. Luke's plays an active role in Long Beach's Gay Pride Festival. Some of our straight parishioners take part because they try to live by the Golden Rule. Others are seeking to *right a wrong*. Still others *value the differences* among us and give thanks for the enrichment that diversity brings to our parish. We have a booth at the Festival. We celebrate the Eucharist before the parade. We march in the parade. In part, we walk in the parade as a public witness to show that we, as gay and straight Christians, are allies of the LGBT community. As I discovered the first time I took part in the parade, to walk also means being an ally in another way.

At one point in the parade, there is always a group of Christian hecklers stationed to shout out slogans, Bible verses, and curses. While the rest of the parade is festive, these shrill voices from the side of the road yell through megaphones that gays are going to hell. When the hecklers see religious leaders walk by, they shout that we are worse than our gay parishioners. We are going to hell for deceiving our parishioners, for allowing gays and lesbians to be who they are.

It is an interesting thing to be told that you are going to hell. For my gay parishioners, this form of spiritual abuse is the norm, a verbal form of being spit on. For me, it comes only with being an ally and only when it is known that I am an ally. Being an ally can mean risking retaliation, even so mild as verbal abuse. In the old South, whites who sought minimal decency for blacks were called n—— lovers. Sometimes physical violence follows verbal violence. After 9/11, religious leaders who banded together with American Muslims in opposition to vigilantism sometimes risked becoming targets as well. Being an ally means being willing to share the risk sometimes that others face all of the time.

Understanding Others

If we are to be allies, one of the requirements is that we understand the people with whom we are aligning ourselves. We have to ask ourselves what being an "ally" really means from *their* perspective. At St. Luke's, where we have various programs that respond to our homeless neighbors, we have to ask ourselves: What does it mean to become an ally of homeless people as a group, not just each homeless individual who comes to us for food or to take a shower? An ally would learn about the causes of homelessness. An ally would take part in attempts to minister to and with homeless persons. Further, an ally would seek to end homelessness as a structural societal problem.

What does it mean to become an ally of members of a racial group other than your own? Minimally, an ally would learn history and sociology. What would it mean to be an ally of a member of the Nation of Islam? What would it mean to be an ally of an undocumented immigrant? In a more general way, we need to develop a contemplative awareness of all people of other faiths, races, cultures, and classes. Contemplation is not a compartmentalized area of life apart from the harsh realities of the world. It is a way of seeing, of being fully awake and completely alive in the world, aware of the sparks of divinity in every created thing, and equally aware of the debilitating and corrupting power of evil in the world.

Thich Nhat Hanh speaks about developing a "non-toothache" awareness.[14] When you have a toothache, you can think of nothing else but that tooth. Your consciousness and emotional energy are directed and entirely absorbed. Having a non-toothache awareness, then, suggests that we can develop that same level of attention toward all of life. I especially like the term because it applies doubly to those who are over-privileged in any way. As a straight person, I do not daily experience the anxiety of gay people who wonder when homophobia will next take another nick out of their souls. As a white person, I do not hourly experience subtle and blatant forms of stereotyping, prejudice, and discrimination. As a man, I do not have to wonder how my voice will be heard in the corridors of power. To have those negative experiences is to live with a toothache. You cannot help but think about it. *Not* to have those experiences on a daily basis means that we must cultivate a non-toothache awareness about the pain of others. It is the *zaddik's* empathetic pain for the woman in labor who is fifty miles away; it is the spiritual work of becoming an ally.

Understanding others requires us to know something of their history, but Americans have a peculiarly ahistorical view of the present, as if it were hermetically sealed off from the past. Continuity, however, is far more often the truth about history. To take just one example, there is a terrible theme and variation in race relations through time. Frederick Douglass wrote that his slave masters wanted their slaves to fight and drink instead of learning how to read.[15] Today, our social systems unwittingly seem to encourage drug use and violence in the inner cities instead of pouring resources into schools and libraries. It is the same dynamic Douglass described, merely refined, less personal, but no less destructive.

Just as we need to be aware of continuities through time, we must also acknowledge that events can change the way we perceive history. Our understanding of the history of slavery is altered by the triumph of abolitionism. Our understanding of race relations is changed because of the progress toward equality that the Civil Rights movement achieved one hundred years later.

Yet unfinished progress toward racial equality does not undo the horror of slavery, something that white Americans should never forget. Slavery gave way to discrimination, Jim Crow laws, and lynching. When one heinous form of evil ends, further steps toward—and away from—equality continue.

It is important to recognize that what happens in the *present* can help bring resolution to what happened in the *past*. What we do today can rewrite the meaning of our lives. While our Christian tradition tends to have a more linear sense of time than Eastern Religions, we still pray for those who have died. We seek to forgive as God forgives us. Both can change our perceptions of the past: They can alter the past so that it no longer has the power to enslave us.

Emptying Ourselves

Part of becoming an ally requires that we empty ourselves— or be emptied by grace, of all obstacles and blinders. For those from dominant positions in society, this *kenosis* (Greek for "emptiness") means the emptying of privilege. For the majority of people in the world, it means facing and emptying oneself of humiliation and disgrace.

A. J. Muste, an American activist and pacifist, once said that there is a gulf between those who have experienced humiliation *as a people* and those who have not.[16] Both the collective experience of humiliation and the absence of such an experience can be a stumbling block to entering diversity as equals. While acknowledging and even measuring the abyss, an over-privileged ally can understand the experience only secondhand, if at all; for those who have felt the direct sting of humiliation, the obstacle is the firsthand stain of disgrace and shame.

There is a strange and beautiful story in the Mahabharata, one of the Hindu scriptures. Yudhisthira was the eldest of the five Pandava brothers, who were all married to the same woman, Draupadi. Yudhisthira once gambled in a game of dice with a man named Sakuni, who kept cheating and winning. Yet Yudhisthira unwisely bet on one thing after another: his pearls, his gold and silver, a thousand elephants, his royal chariot drawn by eight horses white as moonbeams, a thousand maids skilled in singing and dancing, and a thousand male servants. He lost each in turn. Finally, Yudhisthira risked losing his wife, Draupadi, who worked harder than any servant, yet was as "fragrant as the lotus . . . a woman that any man would desire for a wife—compassionate and sweet-tongued . . . Even when her face drips with sweat she resembles jasmine."

As Yudhisthira made the bet, onlookers cried out, "Shame! Shame!"

But it was too late. With another roll of the dice, Draupadi belonged to Sakuni's master, the Pandava brothers' archenemy.

As is so often the case, the shame that should have been Yudhisthira's became the humiliation of Draupadi. She was brought out and forced to disrobe in front of her new master and his accomplices. Because she was menstruating, she was dressed in only one piece of cloth that wrapped around her, exposing her navel.

But when Draupadi prayed to the gods to deliver her from her disgrace, the god Krishna "caused another garment to appear where one was stripped off." Each time Sakuni's crony, Dussasana, tried to strip off one cloth, another of lovely colors appeared underneath so that soon the floor was covered with many-hued dresses. The one cloth was miraculously multiplied so that many garments, each more beautiful than the one before, covered Draupadi and spared her the disgrace her opponents sought to wreak on her.

As the cloths kept appearing, the witnesses began to sense that they were in the presence of a miracle, and they turned on those who would humiliate her: "A murmur arose among the assembled kings which grew into a roar of anger against Dussasana," the accomplice seeking to strip Draupadi.

Dussasana was revealed as nothing more than a lackey, and he "sat down ashamed," bearing the weight of the humiliation intended for the woman.[17]

I first heard this story in a sermon by Winnie Varghese, who told it in response to the 1998 Lambeth Conference statement on sexuality. The Lambeth Conference, which brings together the world's Anglican bishops, meets once every ten years at the invitation of the Archbishop of Canterbury. While Lambeth has no power to legislate for the Anglican Communion, its statements carry a moral weight and sometimes a burden. In 1998, the bishops wrote a statement that condemned same-sex relationships "as incompatible with Scripture," while hypocritically claiming that the church could still respond to the pastoral needs of gay and lesbian persons. In that light, the point of Winnie's sermon was bold: No matter what people, including the church, do to humiliate you, God will not let you be ashamed. Instead, God will shame those who seek to shame you.

A similar message was delivered to the Jewish people after they had returned from their exile in Babylon and resettled in Jerusalem. They had been defeated two generations before, their temple desecrated, pillaged and burned, their royal family murdered, and their leaders carted off on a degrading journey to Babylon. Now, however, they were promised through the prophets that they would never be dishonored again; that, in fact, their past disgrace had been transformed. God had arranged for a *kenosis*, an emptying, of their humiliation, and the prophets comforted God's people (Isa 40:1):

Do not fear, for you will not be ashamed; do not be discouraged, for you will not suffer disgrace; for you will forget the shame of your youth, and the disgrace of your widowhood you will remember no more. (Isa 54:4; see also 25:8)

Arise, shine; for your light has come, and the glory of
the Lord has risen upon you. . . . Then you shall see
and be radiant; your heart shall thrill and rejoice. . . .
The nations shall see your vindication, and all the
kings your glory; you shall be called by a new name
that the mouth of the Lord will give. . . . You shall no
more be termed Forsaken, and your land shall no more
be termed Desolate; but you shall be called My Delight
Is in Her, and your land Married; for the Lord delights
in you. (Isa 60:1, 5; 62:2, 4)

The tale of Draupadi also has similarities with the story of
Esther, who interceded for her people as Draupadi prayed for
herself. While the conniving Haman sought both to humiliate and to exterminate the Jewish people, Esther exposed the
conspiracy to King Ahasuerus. Haman then suffered the fate
he had intended for the Jews, just as Dussasana endured the
shame originally directed at Draupadi.

Jesus, too, often erased people's disgrace and transferred
it to those who, through their judgmentalism, had targeted
others for shame. Perhaps the most obvious example is the
story of the woman caught in adultery. Jesus' wise statement, "Let any one of you who is without sin be the first
to throw a stone at her" (Jn 8:7), not only started to set her
free, but also forced the crowd of men around her to face
their own guilt.

The founding Christian memory is filled with the healing
of disgrace, whether the shame was externally orchestrated
or internally perpetuated, whether it came from status or sin.
When Simon the Pharisee sneered at the woman of Bethany,
Jesus compared her generous actions favorably against his
penurious hospitality. Instead of allowing Simon to humiliate her, Jesus used her actions to shame, and awaken, Simon
(Lk 7:36–50). Her disgrace was healed. Just as Jesus healed
the hemorrhaging woman (Mk 5:25–34), which would have

been a shameful ailment in her culture, he also turned around and erased the disgrace of Zacchaeus, the first-century equivalent of the corrupt CEO. In his letters, Paul, too, carried on this tradition and insisted that those who believed in Jesus would not be put to shame (Rom 9:33, 10:11).

When both kinds of *kenosis* occur, the blotting out of shame and the self-emptying of privilege, there is room for the oppressed and the oppressors, for the under- and the over-privileged, to come together in harmony. Isaiah's vision—that there would come a time when Assyria and Egypt would also be God's people alongside the people of Israel—was a vision of conquerors and oppressors living in harmonious equality with those they had so horribly demeaned. Yet this vision of the lion, the wolf, the bear, and the asp living in peace with the lamb, the calf, the ox, and the nursing child (11:6–8) has been parodied into the saying, "The wolf may lie down with the lamb, but the lamb won't get much sleep."[18] Just so, diverse communities need to acknowledge that as they come together there is always an imbalance of privilege and power. Some enter with a history of being wolves, others as lambs, and both need the self-emptying of the past in order to become bread to each other.

For those who have felt the sharp edge of scapegoating and stereotyping, this immediately and obviously comes as good news. The overwhelming human tendency is to internalize messages of disgrace, all too similar to the ways children absorb verbal abuse. When one is barraged by propaganda within one's society or within one's family, it is hard to escape its effects. Yet as the Syrophoenician woman allowed that, yes, maybe others saw her as a dog, she declared that even dogs got their crumbs.

For those who have not felt the knife-edge of humiliation as a people, it is critical that when asked, "Who is my neighbor," the answer be specific. My neighbor is the Samaritan, the one who has been abused by the religious and ethnic norms of the times, the one whose experience of life is very different from mine. With this admission comes the beginning of being forgiven, of having one's past sins emptied of their power.

Moving toward Reconciliation

If the goal is constant union with God, and unending and extraordinary unity with our neighbor, how do we know when we get there? It is dangerous to think that we are too close to the goals of our life, to holiness or perfect compassion. In John Bunyan's *The Pilgrim's Progress*, Christian and Christiana traveled an allegorical road and neared the end of their journey in a place called the Enchanted Ground.[19] Here the pilgrims, sluggish with complacency, fell asleep tragically close to their destination.

Those who think they have reached spiritual maturity because they no longer tell sexist or homophobic or ethnic jokes, or that they are racially self-realized because they are "color blind," or who "tolerate" gays, lesbians, Muslims, and Hindus, are, in fact, still limping along between two opinions. They have not yet understood that they are equals with the people they tolerate.

"Toleration" is merely another form of condescension, a less odious way of expressing one's superiority. It is like lowering oneself from a fourteenth-floor penthouse but still looking down from a third-floor suite. The angle may not be as steep, but the operative word is still "down."

Sometimes in their spiritual path, conservatives look no further than the interpersonal level because to go beyond that would require a complete conversion in the way they see the world. They still strain gnats and swallow camels. Sometimes in their path, liberals focus solely on the social, structural level. They have washed the outside of the cup with an ideology, but they have not incorporated the spirit into their hearts or an interpersonal practice into their daily lives. As John Bunyan would remind us, on this path there is no place to stop.

Yet we do stop too early. In the Christian tradition, we talk about reconciliation, the holding or bringing together of humanity with God, of one person or one group of people with another. We create justice and practice forgiveness in order to make reconciliation possible, but this does not mean that we throw forgiveness to the wind and expect it to do the work by itself.

There are true and false kinds of reconciliation, an important distinction in contemporary Anglicanism when some people use the word "reconciliation" as a way to preserve the status quo.

One of my former parishioners marched in Selma in 1965 during the voter registration drive. As an African-American Episcopalian, he attempted to attend the local segregated Episcopal church on Sunday and was turned away at the door. He went with others to see the Bishop of Alabama and was told that the diocese was working on reconciliation. He pointedly asked the core question: "How can you have reconciliation when some people are inside, and others are kept outside?"

We need to keep asking the same question. How can there be reconciliation with those within the church who still deny the validity of the ordination of women without pushing women away from the altar? How can there be reconciliation within the church when some are performing same-sex marriages and blessing gay unions while others disagree? Reconciliation can only begin when all are inside the door and treated equally at the altar.

There is a long and hopeful lineage of the privileged becoming allies of the dispossessed. White abolitionists sought an end to the slavery of African Americans. Under Nazi occupation a few—too few—Christians risked and lost their lives to save their brother and sister Jews from persecution. A majority of men in Congress voted for women's suffrage. Peoples of every race joined with African Americans during the Civil Rights movement, seeking justice and racial reconciliation. Yet those with power need always to be mindful that they are not unconsciously seeking to seize the reins for their own ends.

Moving toward God means that, ultimately, we will become *allies of creation*. In the kabbalistic tradition, *tikkun* (mending) begins with a myth of creation in which God has to withdraw to make room for creation in order for creation to come into being. A vacuum is left behind surrounded by divine light, and the light emanates into vessels that shatter because they cannot contain the divinity. The shattered vessels fall to the world, and divine shards fill every created thing.[20] These innumerable pieces become divine sparks in creation that need to be redeemed. It is the work of the *zaddik* to awaken to, relate to, and redeem those sparks in every person, every creature, and every thing.

In some ways, this tradition is similar to the view of Hinduism that there is something of Krishna in all created things; and to the Christian view that there is something of the Logos, the Word, in all created matter (Col 1). In the Jewish tradition of *tikkun*, everything we do—each small action—either mends or tears at the fabric of creation.

This, in turn, is similar to Buddhist tradition that says our almost unnoticeable sins of omission or commission are like drops of water collected in a jar. After a while, there is enough water not only to fill the jar, but to drown in it. On the other hand, every act of love also fills us, drop by drop, until we are full of love.[21] This "inter-being," as it is called in Buddhism, is an extraordinary unity with our Creator.

John of the Cross, one of the most sophisticated of all Christian spiritual writers, offered a simple but profound aphorism for our complex world: "Where there is no love, put love, and there you will find love."[22]

In other words, do not wait for someone else to fill the world with love. Do not wait for others to become allies. Where there is a vacuum, fill it.

This is no simple task, yet it is far more difficult if one substitutes the word "justice" for "love": where there is no justice, put justice, and there you will find justice. While love is an interpersonal action, justice requires collaboration, organization, grassroots action, mass movements, and social change. While it may be hard to love an individual, or to dive into cold river water to save a drowning stranger, it is far more complex to know what to do—or even what to think—when people are being herded together outside your apartment in a village square, or when you hear about prisons or poverty or systemic racism or ethnic cleansing or war.

If we are going to show love to neighbor and stranger, if we are to "strive for justice and peace" for every human being, we need to take a spiritual inventory. What steps do we need to take to reorient our lives so that we can be allies of the poor, of people of a different sexual orientation, of people of other faiths, and of people of other races? How are we to do justice to them concretely as people whose lives are deeply affected by the systems and structures of our time? What are their public interests? What public policies and laws serve their needs? Which ones violate their dignity and their integrity? Which ones undermine hope? Which ones shame them? Which ones could diminish their shame and spark hope?

It is by loving others enough to become their allies that the odor of sanctity begins to emanate from us. When we do justice, we begin to become bread.

Spiritual Exercise: Wheat and Chaff

When grain is gathered at harvest time into bundles, hundreds of shafts of wheat, small grains, and kernels become mixed up with the chaff, the seed-coverings that are ultimately discarded. It is only on very close examination that you can tell wheat from chaff.

Look at the illustration of the Wheat and the Chaff. Imagine a stack that holds together all of your experiences of people different from yourself (both positive and negative), all of your stereotypes, the times you have shamed others and the times that you have been disgraced. The stack includes your thoughts, words, and deeds toward people different from you. Some have been wonderful and illuminating; others have been destructive.

To help separate the Wheat from the Chaff, take some time to reflect on the following questions.

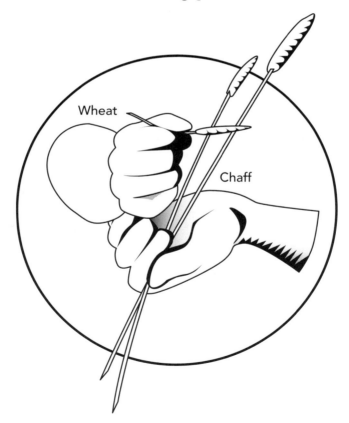

The chaff includes the negative things we can transform and, when we examine them, can transform us. Make a list of your answers to these questions under the word "Chaff."

- What are the ways you have hurt and disgraced others as members of a group?
- What do you need to forgive yourself—or someone else—for?
- What are the things you have done to others that need to be healed?
- What are the disgraces you have endured that need to be healed?

Now make a list of your answers to the following questions under the word "Wheat."

- What in your life, and in yourself today, is the wheat that can be turned into bread?
- What are the positive experiences you have had of people different from yourself?
- What have you done, or could you do, to learn about yourself and others so that you grow in empathy for people with experiences different from your own?
- What are some ways that you have acted as an ally to others?
- In what ways are you an ally to others today?

When you sift through the positive and negative things in yourself, you are practicing purgation and preparing yourself for illumination and union.

Spiritual Counsel

Meditate on one of the following quotations each day during the next week. As you do so, ask yourself these questions:

- How does this touch my heart?
- How does it affect the way I wish to interact with people I meet, especially people of a different gender, sexual orientation, religion, or race?
- How does it help me see large groups of people, especially people of other nations, cultures, races, and religions?

"How long will you go limping with two different opinions?"—1 Kings 18:21

"Do not fear, for you will not be ashamed; do not be discouraged, for you will not suffer disgrace; for you will forget the shame of your youth, and the disgrace of your widowhood you will remember no more."—Isaiah 54:4

"First take the log out of your own eye, and then you will see clearly to take the speck out of your neighbor's eye." —Matthew 7:5

"A mouse does not forgive a cat while the cat is mauling the mouse."—Gandhi

"Where there is no love, put love, and there you will find love."—John of the Cross

Spiritual Practice

Do one or more of these practices in the next week.

- Study a controversy from the past on an issue of race, gender equality, sexual orientation, class, or religion. In terms of religion, you might choose the Crusades. Regarding race, you might study discriminatory laws *outside* the South. In terms of class, you might study a chapter in the history of the labor movement. Regarding sexual orientation, you might consider the history of criminalizing sex between adults of the same sex. As you learn about the controversy, decide which side you would have taken on this issue in the past. Then read about a parallel issue today. Which side are you on now, and how does taking this side show that you are an ally of someone different from yourself?

- Make a list of resolutions of things you can do to become and to practice being a person completely open to the gift of human diversity. Make sure your list helps to answer these questions: How can I be your ally? How can I be bread for others?

- At the end of each day this week, ask yourself, "How have I been bread for people like me?" Then ask yourself, "How have I been bread for people different from me? How have I been an ally?"

CHAPTER 5
Rainbow Communities

WHEN I was in campus ministry in the 1980s, the University Religious Center had an ecumenical Ash Wednesday service each year hosted by the Roman Catholic Church. A majority of those who attended were Catholic, but the rest of us from the URC and nearby churches invited our own students and parishioners. The Christian clergy of the URC—primarily Catholic, Episcopal, Lutheran, Presbyterian, American Baptist, and Methodist—planned the service together. Each preacher took a turn in the pulpit. One year, after taking part in three such Ash Wednesday services, a particularly well-read and theologically astute graduate student complained to me that not once in the years he had attended the ecumenical Ash Wednesday service had he heard anything about sin or repentance.

It was true. The URC "made nice" on Ash Wednesday, just as we made nice the rest of the time to avoid serious issues or differences. We had so many low-level, ongoing personality conflicts that our avoidance of each other led us to avoid any differences or controversies, which even led us to avoid any mention of sin. The URC looked good on paper, but a paltry few good things came out of our practice.

This graduate student perceptively pointed out, "If you're not going to talk about sin on Ash Wednesday, why not use the ashes to put happy faces on our foreheads instead of crosses?"

This was constructive theological and liturgical criticism of an ecumenical group that had so watered down its message than even when it ought to have found common ground, it skated above it in an ethereal Never-never-land. A completely different dynamic was more often at work. After the service, inevitably a few Episcopalians would gather in a corner of a room or the parking lot and re-examine every word and action of the liturgy, like chimpanzees delighting in picking through each other's hair. The criticisms flowed freely, usually along the lines of *"That* simply wasn't well done," or, "It would have been better if *we* had planned it."

While the graduate student's comments about the content of the service had been helpful, this narcissistic, frivolous, and aloof critique of style was hurtful. Many of us have a hard time differentiating between content and style, between the essential and the superfluous, between our primary and secondary beliefs. Yet this is a critical issue in any healthy community—especially in a diverse or ecumenical one. Building a community according to a shared vision is essential. Picking at a community because not everything is from our "well" or is consistent with our life experience or theology is counterproductive.

In order to create a productive multifaith group or a multicultural community, people need to both *envision* and *embody* diversity. The URC had begun with a vision, but it had a hard time embodying it. In any pluralistic community it is preferable, in theory, to envision before trying to embody, but reality is rarely so linear. In some ways, it is hard to envision diversity until one has begun to embody it. It is also hard to embody a vision that has not been articulated. Neither step need be completed before starting the other. Both go side by side.

Envisioning Diversity

There is no more important role for leaders in a diverse community than to cultivate and continually reiterate a clear *vision*, a sense of the *meaning* of the community, a clarity about why the community exists and what it seeks to achieve. At first, such a vision might be a vague outline, as something seen through a thin mist on a distant horizon. As people draw closer to it, the contours get clearer. Without this kind of communal spiritual direction, it is next to impossible to become a healthy diverse community. Even when the vision is clearly delineated, congregations struggle to balance their vision, vocation, and identity against their anxiety about survival.

Vision helps any movement toward justice, equality, and inclusion to coalesce. In 1959, as Martin Luther King, Jr. gave a speech in Washington D.C. during an event that foreshadowed the famous March on Washington four years later, he said that what he saw in that racially integrated crowd was "the face of the future."[1] In South Africa during the last years of apartheid, when Archbishop Desmond Tutu spoke to racially mixed crowds, he said that he saw "the rainbow people of God."[2] Unlike rainbows in the sky, which are always seen from a distance and can never be entered or touched, *rainbow communities* can both be seen and experienced.

The rainbow is an old and a new symbol of diversity and hope. Today it is a symbol of the LGBT community as well as of racial harmony. The first rainbow in the Bible is the colorful skywriting that announced to Noah and to all the creatures on the ark that a new day in creation had dawned. It was time to refill the earth with God's blessings. Whenever the rainbow would appear in the sky, it would remind God of this covenant with all creatures. It would remind all creatures of God's unconditional commitment to work with creation until God's will is done on earth as in heaven. From its beginning in our religious tradition, the rainbow is a forward-looking symbol of hope.

Biblical visions of different kinds of "rainbows" followed the story of Noah's Ark. Isaiah's invitation to all who thirst (55:1), like Jesus at the well with the Samaritan woman—or the hope that Jews, Egyptians, Assyrians, and Samaritans can come together—are memories we need emblazoned in our hearts. Isaiah's vision that those who had been excluded from the covenant because of their sexual, ethnic, or national identity would be included should be written on every signpost in our congregations. As Isaiah said, when God is finished gathering in these outcasts, God will welcome more (56:8)! Maybe it will be people of another class or another faith, perhaps people more conservative in their politics or more liberal in their theology. Maybe it will be people who speak a different language or whose household looks different from our own. Both Isaiah and Micah envisioned all of the nations coming to Jerusalem to learn and, alongside the people of Israel, to walk in God's ways. In the Book of Revelation, there are visions of peoples coming from all nations to the New Jerusalem to gather around the throne of God. Each time we say the Lord's Prayer, we unleash the vision of the Kingdom of God on earth as it is already seen in the mind of God.

Yet for those whose experience is primarily one of homogeneity (one color of the rainbow), it can be hard to envision a rainbow. While it might be easier to envision racial diversity in a diverse megalopolis, it may be more difficult in a suburb, a gated community, or a small town. Even within a congregation that is beginning to experience cultural diversity, there are legitimate—even anxious—questions that need to be answered: How can we embrace diversity without losing our identity, the things that give us spiritual sustenance? Or in an ecumenical or interfaith context: How can we embrace religious diversity without making of relativism a vapid, iconoclastic god?

Many fear that their "well" may become diluted or polluted. Yet holding onto homogeneity is simply a modern form of tribalism that encourages us to remain spiritually impoverished and immature. To remain in our religious or cultural or sexual ghettoes would be to insist, to paraphrase Paul, that when we become adults, we stay children. In churches, we notice if there are no children or no youth or no families or no seniors. Why do we not notice that there is no racial or cultural diversity? Why do we not notice that there are no same-sex couples? Members of homogeneous churches are spiritually deprived of an incredible opportunity for spiritual growth. Yet it takes a focused effort to face the spiritual issues that go with a heterogeneous congregation. That spiritual exploration begins with the articulation of a clear vision.

Each rainbow community develops in its own ways— quickly in some areas, slowly in others—especially when a congregation is not building on years of intentional preparation and practice. When I came to the parish at St. Luke's, I encountered a history of resistance to cultural diversity. While the immediate neighborhood had been predominantly Spanish-speaking for two decades, there had never been a commitment to open the church's doors to its neighbors. A few people in the parish wanted the church to welcome its Spanish-speaking neighbors, but because the overall history had not prepared the soil for planting or growth, I knew there had to be a phase of preparation before they could envision the church as a rainbow community.

A few small steps had already been taken. Prior to my arrival, the vestry had given their approval to a group of parishioners to visit five bilingual parishes in the diocese to learn how they started their Spanish services and how they practiced a bilingual common life. When we started to broach the subject of starting a service in Spanish, I met with the vestry for a focused meeting and found that they had adopted the same cross-armed posture (literally) that I had encountered when I had mentioned stewardship earlier. While they asserted that Latinos might not have our traditions and might not be self-supporting members of the church, they did not want to talk about their own stewardship!

I thought that an inductive, non-directive discussion would be the least threatening. I was wrong. It didn't work at all. We floundered. At our next regular meeting, I asked what could have been more constructive. They said they needed more reasons *why* we—as Christians—should become bilingual and *how* we would become bilingual. In other words, in order to *envision* the future, they needed to have a sense of what it would look like. They had not yet even begun to *imagine* that there was another horizon, let alone discern any of its details.

So when I led a parish forum two months later about starting a service in Spanish, not only did I give ten reasons for diversity (see Chapter 2), I also gave ten steps we could take:

1. Develop funding from within the parish, perhaps with diocesan support, to hire the staff necessary to begin this ministry.
2. Work within the congregation to create the spiritual depth necessary to be a truly welcoming congregation.
3. Offer opportunities for diversity training within the congregation.
4. Offer Spanish classes for parishioners.
5. Develop community programs at St. Luke's that are led in Spanish.
6. Make one of our outreach programs bilingual.

7. Start programs on the premises that reach out to Spanish-speaking families.
8. Invite existing Spanish-speaking community groups to meet at St. Luke's.
9. Develop Spanish-speaking house churches in the neighborhood.
10. Put up banners in Spanish when the time came to start Spanish worship services.

Because at that point we lacked the human and financial resources to push ahead with any speed, the horizon seemed hypothetical and that helped alleviate anxieties. Nevertheless, I hoped that some concrete ideas would enable people to envision that such a future could come into being. Though the list was hardly a be-all or end-all, it seemed to assuage people's doubts, and it encouraged the vestry to make this a long-range goal. It traced a feasible path and enabled people to see what the distant horizon *might* look like.

When I had been at St. Luke's for three years, we initiated a process that allowed for broad participation in the formation of a vision statement. We put a "ballot box" in the parish hall for several weeks in which parishioners could leave notes about what they believed was or ought to be the essence of St. Luke's. We held a class during the Easter season that read through the Gospel of Luke and ended each evening answering the question: What would a community based on this Gospel be like? The data from both sources was recorded for the vestry to review and digest.

Then the vestry met together for a day to brainstorm and came up with sixty different key words, which were put up on a board. Then, gradually, they edited and revised their way to the most central words to articulate who we were and what we wanted to be. There was a fruitful discussion about how the LGBT community and persons of color would respond to words such as "diverse," "inclusive," and "multicultural." It was a thoughtful, respectful, and creative discussion, and with some follow-up to polish the words, we clarified our vision as: "an inclusive, multicultural community pursuing spiritual and social transformation." We had also discussed the need to have a specific mention of Jesus, which some vestry members felt had been missing in St. Luke's spiritual life in the recent past. So we added a logo statement: "following Jesus' loving example." Both the vision statement and the logo statement provided healthy spiritual direction for the congregation and also gave prospective seekers a glimpse of our church's identity.

Ultimately, congregations that choose to welcome diversity as a spiritual gift need such a vision. When I was graduating from seminary and interviewing for a job at a church, I asked the vestry what they saw happening in their church in the next few years. There was a long awkward silence until one person said, "Growth." For many congregations, the goal of the church is to survive or thrive (in undefined ways). Even those congregations that have made the effort to write a vision statement have sometimes created banal and forgettable declarations.

Tragically, many congregations have no vision at all. Or, like the early Christian community in Laodicea in the Book of Revelation, their visions are lukewarm. They bear no fruit; they neither help nor harm; and by doing so, they cripple themselves with their blandness (Rev 3:15–16). If a church has a vision statement that does not have something particular to its mission, its social location, its theological sensibility, its town or neighborhood or city, its sense of *place*, that church has no vision. Congregations need statements that speak to their environments; they need an incarnational vision, or they should not bother.

A vision statement provides an integrating principle that memorably sums up the primary purpose of an organization. The statement needs to be succinct and unique. If it is not a strong statement of a particular identity, then our faith communities become subject to inertia and routine. Instead of being a witness to other faith communities and to organizations of the possibilities of having a profound vision and a unique identity, they become, in the terminology of Hebrew scriptures, like all the other "nations," not understanding their unique relationship with God.

Embodying Diversity

While envisioning is critical to the formation of rainbow communities, the Christian faith is incarnational, not a set of good ideas. Until visions become enfleshed in institutions, they float uselessly like wispy clouds in our imaginations. Vision without embodiment is like dreaming that we are running. Embodiment is part of our ecclesiology, our theology of the church.

Throughout history, there have always been mini-societies seeking to embody an envisioned future. Intentional communities are nothing new. In Christian history, many different kinds of intentional communities have formed with a common commitment to deepen personal spiritual development by living together: the communities of desert Christians in the fourth and fifth centuries, the monastic communities of the Middle Ages, and the gathered Protestant communities of the Radical Reformation. In American history, the Shakers were but one example of a long tradition of utopian experiments in communal living.

In the last century, the ecumenical religious community at Taize, France, was formed to welcome all seekers, especially young adults, and to bring people together from many and from no religious background. Gandhi's ashram in India, and before that his ashram in South Africa, brought together people of different races and religions to share a common life and to model the way peoples of different cultures and castes could live together in creative equality. In southwest Georgia in the 1940s, Clarence Jordan founded the Koinonia Farm, an intentional community seeking to practice racial equality in what he hoped would be the future of the American South.[3] The Catholic Worker houses of hospitality and cooperative farms were intended to cross class lines as the voluntarily poor and the involuntarily poor mixed together. Howard Thurman, an African-American religious leader of the mid-twentieth century, served at the interdenominational Church for the Fellowship of All Peoples, a purposefully integrated congregation in San Francisco.

All five of these intentional communities shared a commitment to embody a vision of equality and integration. These rainbow communities did not stand off to the side and simply radiate light. They engaged the world with the values that emerged from the content of their common life. All five communities carried on the tradition of being "schools of charity," like the monastic communities of Benedict. In each one, people learned how to love one another in the course of living, working, worshipping, and praying together, bumping into and bruising each other, and finding reasons to deepen the reality of reconciliation. That is not to say that each one was, or is, a successful utopian experiment or the kingdom of heaven on earth, but each one partially embodied its vision. That, by itself, is a tremendous achievement.

Embodying our vision requires *intentionality*, the determination to bring ideals into being. A community must *choose* to be diverse. Individuals must *choose* to be a part of a diverse community. There are hundreds of urban churches that have not wanted to adapt when their neighborhood demographics shifted. I have heard people imply (though they rarely put it this way out loud), that they would rather have their congregation die than see it change. While commitment to diversity might require less in a multicultural church, where one attends only on Sundays, than in an ashram or a

Catholic Worker house or the Koinonia Farm, where it is a 24/7 commitment, the leadership and the congregation need to be intentional about everything that happens: worship, music, fellowship, education, stewardship—everything that goes into a congregation's life.

Far too often the church has been preoccupied with the rind as if it were the fruit itself. William Stringfellow liked to say that the church actually *is* the church "here and there, now and then."[4] There are moments when the institutional church embodies the spirit of Christ. Like the phenomenon of a rainbow, it is fleeting but no less beautiful for shining bright for only a short time.

The Dimensions of Community

The practice of a rainbow community has many dimensions: *interpersonal, spiritual, communal,* and *structural.* It is several hands coming together intertwining their fingers. To limit the process of embodiment to one arena aborts the cohesion needed to hold all of the groups together during times of confusion or conflict. In a congregation, music and liturgy, leadership, stewardship, fellowship, and Christian formation need to become an integrated whole. In a multifaith organization, structural and interpersonal dimensions are paramount. There is often much discussion about the centrality of *dialogue* in encouraging healthy diversity, and dialogue is an especially important part of intentional planning to foster the *interpersonal* dimension.

Shortly after Holy Faith became bilingual and faced the complexity of cultural diversity, we had several intentional dialogues led by recently trained parishioners. But dialogues alone are hardly enough to create the multiple layers of bonding necessary to an intentional community. Informal events at Holy Faith also spurred relationships that crossed cultural and linguistic barriers. For two years, there was a bilingual weeknight dinner followed by English-only and Spanish-only programs in spiritual formation. While thirty people attended these dinners regularly, we needed a majority of the congregation to have at least some personal experience of parishioners who did not speak their language. Shortly after we started the service in Spanish at Holy Faith, we arranged to have—three weeks in a row—a Spanish-speaking parishioner tell his/her story to the English-speaking service, and an English-speaking parishioner tell his/her story to the Spanish-speaking service (all with interpreters). Personal storytelling helped to humanize the "other" as individuals and also the "others" as a group.

The *spiritual* dimension was largely formed through preaching, teaching, worship, and prayer groups. A prayer group that started as bilingual and evolved into Spanish-only was, although not what had been planned, an important cross-cultural experiment, both for those who participated and for those who simply knew that the attempt had been made. In our experience, people found it a strain to continuously take part in bilingual worship, prayer, dialogues, or classes, so most bilingual programs were one-time events.

Issues of communication were also important. At Holy Faith, partly because of a lack of resources, we were slow to make our newsletter bilingual. Fellowship was easier. Although language still presented a barrier, fellowship events—picnics and fiestas and dinners—helped to instill a sense of a shared, *communal* life.

Perhaps hardest of all were *structural* issues: Who are the people in leadership roles and why? At first, as we tried to make our vestry more representative of the whole congregation, we tended to nominate and elect bilingual Latinos in the congregation. But the bilingual people were not necessarily the natural leaders. We had to find ways to educate African and Latin American immigrants about the structures of parish life, including how much money it takes to keep a congregation going in the U.S. and where the money comes from (you!) to keep it going. We also had to educate American-born vestry members to understand that there was not a universal consensus on middle-class values; Robert's Rules of Order did not descend from Mt. Sinai on stone tablets as a universal commandment for ordering meetings. Even church canons for structuring a vestry were not always suitable for enfleshing the church in our community, either in a multicultural context or in campus ministry, where students were unlikely to be able to fill three-year terms before graduating.

While embodying religious pluralism in a multifaith organization may not be as difficult—because it does not require the multidimensionality of a worshipping congregation—yet there is still the need to identify the common values that hold things together, as well as the need to acknowledge the differences that have to be respected in order to keep things from falling apart.

Potential Missteps in Community Formation

In practice, rainbow communities are as "utopian" as most congregations are "heavenly." Sometimes it *is* a story of the wolf lying down with the lamb, and the lamb not getting much sleep. There are many different ways of envisioning and embodying diversity. There can be many ways to be "right"; there are also all kinds of ways to be "wrong."

One way to be wrong is the *apartheid method*. This keeps cultural groups entirely separate all of the time, perhaps in the belief—certainly true—that people are most comfortable with their own cultural styles of worship and fellowship. While people may be most comfortable this way, this is hardly the best way to form one community under the same roof.

When we started services in Spanish at Holy Faith, there

was a strong bias that the whole congregation needed to be united as one. Anything else reminded African-American parishioners of segregation. Congregations that do not have such a solid experience of bringing different peoples together will probably find it more difficult to be united. In California, there are many stories of Anglo congregations merging, perhaps more because of financial need than intentional commitment, with a Korean-speaking or a Filipino congregation, and later separating again with two great sighs of relief. This is the triumph of ethnic ministry over cultural diversity. At times, it can be the right thing to do, especially if parishioners from the dominant culture expect persons of the "other" culture to assimilate. Yet it is never the preferred goal.

When a congregation becomes bilingual, the church may initially be creating a mission within the parish. But this can initiate an imbalance of power that is hard to rectify later. Rather than seeing it as an outreach program, a community seeking intentional diversity takes the more radical step of welcoming people in. It is not the approach of Jonah going out to others (which was hard enough for the people of Israel to stomach), but the experience of Ruth becoming part of the faith community and, in the process, changing it irrevocably.

Wendell Berry tells the amusing story of an all-white church in Kentucky a few decades ago happily supporting missionaries in Africa until two of the African converts arrived at their door expecting to be welcomed as members in their segregated church.[5] Sometimes Jonah is easier than Ruth.

The second main problem in multicultural congregations is the *British Empire method.* The British Empire was diverse. It included India and other parts of Asia, along with huge chunks of Africa and the Caribbean. It was diverse, but everyone in the Empire knew who was in charge: the people with the power to enforce their will and ways on others, as if they were God's will and God's ways. The Nigerian writer Chinua Achebe has said that British colonialists, missionaries included, approached African cultures as if European culture—not Jesus—were the way, the truth, and the life.[6]

There are congregations in which the cultural diversity *looks* beautiful until one sees the Eurocentric nature of worship, the enclosed cultural circles of fellowship, or the class or racial composition of the leadership. In these congregations, there is no equality, no mutual respect; they are top-down, white- (or whatever racial group was there first) on-top operations. Unfortunately, it is natural that those with the longevity and power in a rainbow community would assume that they should continue to wield the most influence on the direction of the congregation, and feel the least impact of the change. This is how diversity gets distorted—even in the envisioning stage—and we get separate-and-unequal parts of the congregation.

In an era in which many churches like to call themselves "diverse," it is one thing to call a mostly white church with a sprinkling of persons of color (or a mostly straight church with a few gay/lesbian persons) "diverse." This speckling of diversity *may* challenge or re-shape a church's identity. However, it is more likely to encourage a pattern of assimilation in which the minority is asked to leave its "well" at the door.

It is quite another to use the word "diversity" to describe a church like Holy Faith, with its five significant cultural groups, whose demographics almost literally cried out for a redefinition of what it meant to be a church.

The Healthy Community

While the example of one congregation's journey can be very helpful to another, I hesitate to call what Holy Faith was doing a "model," much less a "manual" for how to go about moving healthily into diversity. There are many ways to practice diversity. But models can be useful as long as communities know that the model is malleable and must be enfleshed in the particulars of their changing community. The evolution of embodiment needs to be recognized *as it is taking place.*

While there are not any universally applicable models for developing a rainbow community, there are at least *touch-stones.* Planned and unplanned events go hand-in-hand in creating a new, healthy environment. At Holy Faith, we had several programmatic opportunities for one-on-one conversations, as well as facilitator-led small group dialogues during which people shared something about their culture. For these, trained parishioner-facilitators carefully reviewed rules for dialogue so that each person would be respected and each story honored. Some of these were English-only conversations. Other conversations were bilingual.

But dialogues were only part of the process, since only a small percentage of the congregation took part in structured activities. Even before we enunciated our vision, Holy Faith formed a Cultural Diversity Committee alongside Steward-ship, Christian Education, Finance, and the other staples of a congregation. It was the job of the Cultural Diversity Committee to ensure that congregational life was intentionally diverse. They planned and implemented programs to encourage cultural expressions and to bridge cultural and linguistic barriers.

The Cultural Diversity Committee designed Sunday morning Lenten programs for two successive years. The first year, each of the (conveniently) five cultural groups in the church chose a panel from among them and had a chance to tell others what they valued about their culture. This kind of panel gave everyone a chance to put their best face forward. The second year, feeling that a certain level of trust had been established, the Committee became more daring and asked each cultural group to describe how prejudice was expressed in their culture. There was almost always someone in each group who said there was no prejudice in their culture or nation—even an African American speaking about the U.S., who embarrassed all of the others on the panel. But there were always others ready to confess the flaws in their culture. These two programs of pride and prejudice were educational to everyone. Other topics could have been chosen, but these were good for getting snapshots into each other's hearts.

When the Cultural Diversity Committee stopped meeting after three years, we realized that what had once felt contrived had now become a habit. It had become normal to plan bilingual and culturally specific events, normal to find intentional ways to get to know one another, normal to be bilingual and multicultural. In a diverse community's life, it is normalcy that signals a new step in transformation.

Just as important as programs and dialogues are a community's human resources. Holy Faith was blessed with a number of bilingual young adults who were trained as facilitators for dialogues. Other bilingual parishioners, whatever their first language, helped to interpret the vision to those who felt uncomfortable with diversity. Some who understood the vision but lacked linguistic skills could see how it affected our vocation and our identity as a parish. Still others had a ministry of hospitality and human warmth that required no linguistic skills. Passing the Peace, a primarily nonverbal form of expressing warmth and care to those different from oneself, became a very important part of bilingual services because it was so egalitarian: It required no education or social status or linguistic skills, and all could take part equally.

All of these people putting forth various efforts were our *bridge people*—people who were willing to traverse gaps of ignorance and to become bridges for others. Sometimes the bridge people came from racially mixed households or culturally mixed nations. Yet, sometimes, unexpected people formed the bridges. About a year after we started the service in Spanish at Holy Faith, one vestry member who did not like the direction of the parish, asked that we have a "gripe session," which we entitled—more prosaically—an Open Forum. Here people could vent or ask questions. The two most surprising people to speak that day were an African American and an Anglo, both middle-aged males. Neither one usually spoke much at public gatherings. Neither was noted for his rhetorical skill, but both spoke eloquently in favor of the parish being bilingual—one because of his professional experience working beside Latinos, the other because his Christian faith told him that we ought to worship with people different from us. Not all parishioners had wholeheartedly bought into this forming vision of the parish, but as some became articulate in expressing it, they, in turn, became bridges into the future.

One of the most complex areas of creating a rainbow community is the *communal* one, where the spiritualities of each culture come together. At Holy Faith, one of the areas of parish life that needed the most work was music. Each cultural group had its own music, and for some people, that music crossed from one culture to another. There were the distinctive harmonies and rhythms from the African-American tradition and the West African "choruses" we sang (they are repetitive. like the music from Taize, but with a profound percussive kick).

Some people already have the end of the rainbow within them. I recall sitting next to an African-American friend during a service and noting that she sang the European-American hymns as I did, but when she sang African-American music, her voice changed; she sang it "black," in tone and rhythm. She sang biculturally. Most of us do not.

At our Spanish-speaking services, songs were played on

guitar. These songs were completely different from what we sang in our English-speaking services, where our hymns were accompanied by the organ, typical nineteenth- and twentieth-century fare known to our Anglo, African, and Caribbean parishioners who grew up in Anglican churches. It would have been ridiculous—insulting, even—to have used organ music at the Spanish service.

The statement made would be that "your" music, tradition, and religious culture are not as worthwhile as "ours." *We* are superior; *we* invite you to become *our* guests and to feel at home in *our* home.

Your home? *Your* culture? *Your* music? Worthless!

Music is as primal and visceral as language. It is one of our "wells" because it is so deeply personal and profoundly spiritual. Our music traditions carry within them a deep expression of our most basic human experiences that no other music can convey.

It would be a superficial stereotype to imagine that each person in each culture likes each hymn or song of his/her tradition equally. It is absurd to think that one kind of music is "better" or more "sacred" than another kind. Such assertions are at the root of cultural racism. Some music is more complex harmonically, some more difficult melodically, some more sophisticated rhythmically. It is not that one kind of music is "better"; it is that one style of music has become home, the songs of one's heart, part of one's "well." The other music has to be learned. It is not an inbred taste, but an acquired one. Yet tastes can be learned. I remember some of our Nigerian parishioners telling me how much they enjoyed the music sung in Spanish at our occasional bilingual services.

Holy Faith needed an evolution among its English-speakers from so many cultures. How could we regularly include music from each culture so that everyone knew they were valued equally? It took two years of planning to make the transition. The culmination of our work came from the grassroots when parishioners made an intentional statement of their own.

Behind the scenes and unknown to the clergy, Nigerian women met with a group of Latinas to translate three of the Nigerian choruses into Spanish for the ordination of my bilingual assistant, Anna Olson. Even when we had used the Nigerian choruses at our English service once a month, we had sung them mostly in English—even though the words, rhythm, and music were better wedded in Igbo. Singing them trilingually, as became the custom thereafter, was fascinating because the language, the number of syllables per notes, forced revised rhythms into the music. A new culture was emerging from the many cultures gathered in the congregation, a *parish culture* that acknowledged and welcomed the musical contributions of each culture present, like a rainbow that celebrated each color as equally important to the whole.

The transition from one music culture to another was often clumsy and rarely harmonious; occasionally it was excruciatingly painful. It was intentional, though, and it laid a foundation for a new understanding and practice of music. In our stumbling, flawed embodiment, this was our way of being like the New Jerusalem, welcoming "the glory and honor of the nations" (Rev 21:26).

After a few years of worshipping and living together, there comes a point in the life of a rainbow community when persons of different cultural groups begin to *drink from each other's wells*. At its simplest, this means enjoying each other's music and food and clothes and games (if my only informants had been Nigerians, I would have thought piñatas at birthday parties were an ancient African tradition!). At its more complex, it means taking, molding, and relishing the gifts that different cultures offer the new *parish culture*. No one is left out; everyone is open to tasting some of the water from someone else's well and pouring it into their own. While people are usually more prepared to give of their own culture than to receive from another, in the rainbow community, it is more blessed to receive.

At Holy Faith when bilingual services and meetings became normal, when singing African music at Sunday services became normal, when cultural friction and reconciliation became normal, these were the signs that our congregation had moved from *seeing* diversity as an experiment to *embracing* it as a way of life.

Conflict in Community

In nature, in order for a rainbow to form, there must be a storm and sunlight. Without both, there is no rainbow. Conflict in a diverse community is inevitable, but it is also capable of producing the most amazing rainbows. How we handle conflict is the key.

My experiences with the South Coast Interfaith Council and the Long Beach Interreligious Leaders Association have been very positive, but not always easy. At my very first meeting of the Interreligious Leaders Association, we brought in a facilitator to help us talk about Israel-Palestine. It was hardly an auspicious beginning for my working relationship with the rabbi whose point of view was diametrically opposed to mine. My opinions were also vastly different from those of the conservative Christians present who viewed modern Israel in terms of biblical prophecies about end times. A year later in the same group, there was a fairly heated exchange as the U.S. prepared to invade Iraq. The conflict of opinions never seemed to wane. We developed a Multifaith Exploration Series (quarterly education programs with a diverse panel of speakers), and while our speakers always respected each other, they also directly disagreed.

When we envision a rainbow community, we need to know

that it will be a place where values will conflict. The only way to be in real relationship is to be honest. In spite of the occasionally harsh interactions, we were always better off saying what we thought than sugarcoating—and falsifying—our points of view.

One night at Holy Faith, we had a fascinating book discussion group where, for some reason, we started talking about the appropriateness or inappropriateness of using physical force to discipline a child. The upper-middle-class Anglos were adamant that it was "never" right to strike a child. The middle-class African Americans present tended to agree, but with the caveat that their children and grandchildren were growing up in or near such a violent, drug-filled environment that it would be better to practice corporal punishment than to have their children or grandchildren make even one potentially deadly choice. Some African parishioners who, themselves, did not practice physical discipline (they were too "Americanized") said that others did, and they felt it was a matter of culture, not a universal value. This sparked a lively debate, to say the least! But it was a helpful and a healthy dialogue—and one without resolution.

Within conflict, organizations can take on characteristics of a *crowd* or those of a *community*. In a *crowd*, the group drags down the behavior of each person to its lowest common denominator. In a *community*, the group challenges everyone in it to lift his or her behavior to a higher plateau.[7] Israel's covenant with God made it a community committed to encouraging its people to be holy as their God was holy (Lev 19:2). Jesus taught his followers that, in living together in community, they were to be as merciful as God was merciful, as complete and perfect as God (Lk 6:36, Mt 5:48).

Not all diversity results in this kind of community. Without the interlocking interpersonal, spiritual, communal, and structural dimensions—and the dialogue through which people can safely express their anxieties and frustrations—a diverse congregation can easily become a crowd, or two crowds coexisting unhappily. With prayer, planning, teaching, and practice, a diverse congregation can become a true community. With intentionality, a new community will emerge within the shell of the old.[8]

In rainbow communities, large or small, cultural or religious, all people can grow spiritually from the encounter. Thich Nhat Hanh says that every religious tradition can be reinvigorated by its contact with other faiths.[9] If Christianity paid attention to Buddhism, for instance, the "jewels" of our faith—the essential vision and vocation that all too often become submerged beneath the institutional minutiae—might emerge.[10] Kathleen Norris tells the story of a Christian who took part in a Buddhist-Christian dialogue and reported that he had not heard Christian scholars speaking so personally about their love for Jesus in a very long time.[11] Often multifaith conversations give us not only a deeper appreciation of others; they also remind us of what we most deeply cherish in our own "wells."

In the often-tragic history of interreligious conflict, much of the competitive drive between religions continues unabated. These conflicts, of course, are misplaced. As R. S. Sugirtharajah has written:

> In a multireligious context like ours, the real contest is not between Jesus and other savior figures like Buddha or Krishna, or religious leaders like Mohammed . . . it is between mammon and Satan on the one side, and Jesus, Buddha, Krishna, and Mohammed on the other.[12]

To Sugirtharajah, "Satan" means "structural and institutional violence"; "mammon" refers to "personal greed, avariciousness, accumulation, and selfishness"—the very things Christians renounce. We can fall into the age-old habit and find ourselves in conflict with people of other faiths, and with their faith traditions. Alternately, we can embrace Sugirtharajah's vision. Each religion can retain its uniqueness while finding common ground in opposing the forces in human nature—and in institutional structures—that "corrupt and destroy the creatures of God." We can find common ground in seeking the common good.

If Christians are going to practice the humility Jesus commended, we would do well to imitate the practices of Judaism in honoring "righteous Gentiles" and in articulating our own Noadic covenant. In the Jewish tradition, the Noadic covenant is a way by which all non-Jews can enter into a righteous relationship with God without becoming Jewish. This covenant, like the one with Israel, has its moral demands, although more generic than the demands made on the people of Israel. Peter's speech that followed his dream where God showed him that he "should not call anyone profane or unclean" (Acts 10:28) led to his conversion in his understanding of people from other cultures and traditions. His subsequent speech sounds very much like a Noadic covenant in embryo: "In every nation anyone who fears [God] and does what is right is acceptable to [God]" (Acts 10:35).

For Christians, this could be the foundation for a theology that recognizes and celebrates "righteous non-Christians." Someone who matures in her/his religious tradition may be a much better reflection of God's glory than the infantile or, worse, hostile and xenophobic person who claims an allegiance to Christianity. If the church took this idea seriously, we would celebrate people of every faith, not according to their response to doctrine or even to the person of Jesus. Rather, we would discern their relationship with God based on if they do justice, love kindness, and walk humbly with God (Mic 6:8). Within the U.S., where Christianity has all too often been the wolf among lambs, we would honor others by entering dialogues as equals.

In the mid-twentieth century, the African-American religious leader Howard Thurman traveled to South Asia and was confronted by a Muslim about racial segregation in

North American churches. The Muslim told him that Allah laughed with scorn at our racially segregated churches.[13] He was right. Before Christians poke at the limitations of other faiths, we would do well to remove the proverbial two-by-four from our own eye. We would also do well to humbly observe the experience of others as a source of inspiration for ourselves.

Hope in Community

It was his hajj to Mecca that made the pieces of Malcolm X's conversion fit together. Even on the plane to Mecca, his vision began:

> Packed in the plane were white, black, brown, red, and yellow people, blue eyes and blond hair, and my kinky red hair—all together . . . all honoring the same God Allah, all in turn giving equal honor to each other.

At the airport in Mecca his vision continued.

> Pilgrims from Ghana, Indonesia, Japan, and Russia . . . were moving to and from the dormitory where I was being taken. . . . We reached the dormitory and began climbing up to the fourth, top, tier, passing members of every race on earth. Chinese, Indonesians, Afghanistanians [sic].

Finally, in the middle of the Great Mosque, he saw the fulfillment of his vision.

> [The Kaaba] was being circumambulated by thousands upon thousands of praying pilgrims, both sexes, and every size, shape, color, and race in the world. . . . Some were bent and wizened with age; it was a sight that stamped itself on the brain. I saw incapacitated

pilgrims being carried by others. Faces were enraptured in their faith.[14]

Malcolm's experience seems similar to the vision in Revelation 7 of peoples gathered around God's throne. In seeing people of every race mixing together as equals in Mecca, Malcolm saw the embodiment of the society and the world that was his deepest yearning. No longer would he reserve his message for the members of one race. Not that he softened his message about injustice—his experience of racial equality intensified it—but he had seen something that he had once believed to be a pie-in-the-sky opiate as now within the realm of possibility.

This sense of hope that Malcolm found is something every diverse community can give to those who come into contact with it. Just as people can become bridges, so can communities. A seminarian who visited Holy Faith as a member of a Multicultural Ministry Class returned for two more visits. He saw Holy Faith as a place of hope. If people only knew what was here, he said—the cultural and racial mix intentionally celebrating diversity—it would give them hope that larger communities, our city, our society, and our world could find ways to live together constructively.

In the mid-nineties, when we began to realize the significance of Holy Faith's example of bilingual, multicultural diversity, we approached Episcopal seminaries, inviting them to send students to us for this two-week class. We thought it would be worth their while to see what we were choosing to be, and—by demographic necessity if not by religious conviction—what many more churches would become. By that time, we had worked long enough at envisioning and embodying diversity that we felt we had something to offer others. We didn't realize that part of what we had to offer was hope.

Hope comes from those exhilarating "here and there, now and then" experiences that Stringfellow described as the church. The trilingual Nigerian chorus was but one such example. In my second year at Holy Faith, I remember trying to listen to a conversation in Spanish among three parishioners: Julio from Guatemala, a woman from Trinidad, and a man from Singapore. It was a mini-rainbow before my eyes, speaking in a language I didn't understand, and I stopped, smiled, and marveled that I was blessed to work in such a church. At a church picnic, there was a soccer game with Guatemalans, Nigerians, one Englishman, and a couple of L.A. youth playing together on the same field, finding a common joy in the same game. At the reception following the first Africa Day celebration at Holy Faith, Nigerian parishioners made a point to go outside the parish hall and invite the Spanish-speakers, who were just leaving their later service, into the reception. Soon, the dance floor was a rainbow of peoples from different nations moving to the same rhythm joining in a common celebration.

What if we were to expand on such experiences? What could we envision? What could we embody? If we were to imagine a new Noah's Ark for our time, if we were to focus on what the human family might someday look like, it could be astonishing. Imagine, for instance, an ark carrying two Hindus, two Christians, two Muslims, two Buddhists, two Jews, two who practice a Native American religion, two who practice a classical African religion, two agnostics, and two atheists. Imagine a mix that would include two persons from Africa, two from Asia, two Latinos, two of European descent, two from the Middle East, two of mixed ancestry, two gay and two lesbian persons, and two bisexuals (perhaps they are already on board elsewhere). This ark embodies the future of a rainbow community for the world. Who knows what would develop? This rainbow community, like the first Noah's Ark and the rainbow seen from the Ark, would be a sign of hope to all that encountered it.

When we overcome our inertia with vision—and intentionally form our new vocation and identity around that vision— then we, as communities, become signs of hope to the world.

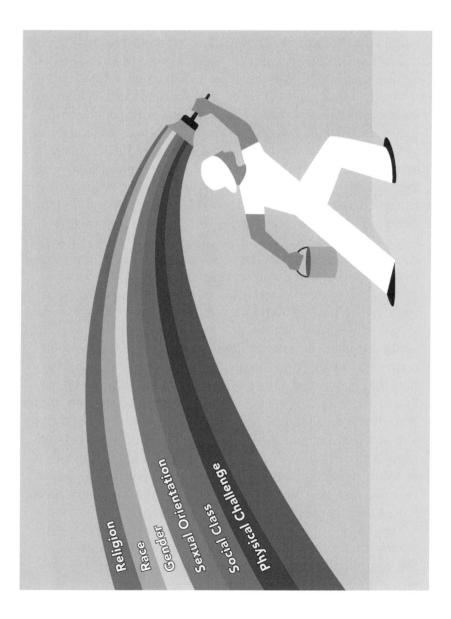

Spiritual Exercise: The Rainbow

In this illustration of a rainbow, each of the six arches represents a different sphere of diversity: religion, race, gender, sexual orientation, social class, physical challenge. Although not visible, each band in this rainbow has within it another rainbow. The religious band, for instance, includes Christians, Jews, Muslims, Sikhs, Buddhists, Hindus, agnostics, atheists, and more. There is the potential for a rainbow of rainbows. Consider what other bands you might add.

- Think of any family, community, group, business, organization, church, neighborhood, school, or college you have been part of that has been diverse in one or more areas.
- How would you identify that community, family, or church: Diverse? Inclusive? Integrated? Multicultural? Multifaith? Interfaith? Bilingual? Other?
- Which areas were diverse? Which areas were not?
- In your experience, was there more intentionality and extra work involved in making that rainbow community work than a homogeneous group?
- How did that rainbow community envision and embody hope for those involved in it? For those who had a tangential experience of it?
- What were the rewards and blessings for you? For others?

Spiritual Counsel

Meditate on one of the following quotations each day during the next week. As you do so, ask yourself these questions:

- How does this touch my heart?
- How does it affect the way I wish to interact with

people I meet, especially people of a different gender, sexual orientation, religion, or race?

- How does it help me see large groups of people, especially people of other nations, cultures, races, and religions?

"When I bring clouds over the earth and the bow is seen in the clouds, I will remember my covenant that is between me and you and every living creature."—Genesis 9:14–15

"Thus says the Lord God, who gathers the outcasts of Israel, I will gather others to them besides those already gathered." —Isaiah 56:8

"After this I looked, and there was a great multitude that no one could count, from every nation, from all tribes and peoples and languages, standing before the throne and before the Lamb."—Revelation 7:9

"People will bring into [the new Jerusalem] the glory and the honor of the nations."—Revelation 21:26

"These are the rainbow people of God."—Desmond Tutu

"The real contest . . . is between mammon and Satan on the one side, and Jesus, Buddha, Krishna, and Mohammed on the other."—R. S. Sugirtharajah

Spiritual Practice

Make a list of the communities of which you are now a part: your home, family, church, neighborhood, town, city, school, university, workplace, and/or volunteer organization. Choose one or more, and ask yourself the following questions:

- In what ways does it already embody the traits of the rainbow?

- In what ways is it yet to embody the traits of the rainbow?
- What steps does it need to take to become a rainbow community?
- What am I willing to do to initiate or help these steps to be taken?

If you do not belong to any "rainbow community," find a diverse worshipping community in your area and visit it. If there are no diverse faith communities near your home, visit one that is of a different faith or culture and/or language than your own. Then ask yourself the following questions:

- How was this experience similar to my usual experience of worship?
- How was it different?
- Were there symbols, expressions of faith, or values to which I could say, "Amen?" What were they?
- How did I feel "at home?" How did I feel excluded?

If you live far from any rainbow communities, use the Internet or your local library to learn about one. Imagine yourself as part of that community and ask yourself the following questions:

- How might I fit in?
- How might I feel part of it?
- What might I find difficult about being part of such a community?
- What might I enjoy?

Epilogue

In Shusaku Endo's last novel, *Deep River*—a story named for the African-American spiritual—Japanese tourists travel to India. The Japanese guide, Enami, has overcome his cultural biases to appreciate India as it is. He tries to explain to the tourists how and why the Indian people see the Ganges River as a holy place. He knows that his compatriots esteem things that appear clean and pure. When he is asked if the Ganges is pure, he replies, "From the Japanese point of view, they couldn't be called clear-flowing rivers in even the polite sense of the term. The Ganga [Ganges] is yellow, and the Yamuna flows grey, and when the two merge, the water turns the color of milky tea. But there is a difference in this country between things that are pretty and things that are holy."[1]

If we want things that seem to us "pretty" or logical or perfect, we will limit ourselves to our own religious and cultural and personal tastes that will probably not even extend or include all points of view within our own religious tradition. We will have what we think we want, but it will not be holy; in fact, it will not be much at all.

If we are willing to extend ourselves, and let our well

flow into the waters of other wells, and let the water from those wells flow into ours, then we will find something truly holy. It will not look the same as it once did. It will not taste the same. It will not immediately feel like home. It will be like that long-ago prayer I said in the hospital at the bed-side of the newly bereaved family I didn't know. That day we found a new rhythm somewhere between my staid, solo Anglican style and their call-and-response style. Its rhythms were awkward. It was not pretty. But it was holy.

What our new, rarely-tried-but-bound-to-be-true prayer will be we have yet to discover. Yet what this meeting of cul-tures, classes, sexual orientations, and religious faiths will become—and what we will become by taking part in the spirit and practice of diversity—is the holiest thing we will ever know.

Notes

Introduction

1. *The Wisdom of the Prophet: Sayings of Muhammad*, 5.
2. Muriel Lester, *Ambassador of Reconciliation*, 174.
3. Dorothy Day, *On Pilgrimage: The Sixties*, 319; *On Pilgrimage*, 53–54.
4. Dorothy Day, *By Little and By Little*, 246.
5. As practiced at the Zen Center in San Francisco.
6. Thomas Merton, *The Other Side of the Mountain*, 323.
7. Martin Buber, *Tales of the Hasidim: Early Masters*, 164.
8. John Climacus, *The Ladder of Divine Ascent*, 289.
9. Martin Buber, quoted in *The Essays of A. J. Muste*, 422.
10. *The Dhammapada*, 21–22. The Dhammapada is a collection of 423 verses containing the Buddha's essential teachings.
11. Peter C. Erb, ed., *Pietists*, 42.
12. *St. Macarius the Spiritbearer*, 30.
13. Kathleen Norris, *Dakota*, 3.

Chapter 1: We Drink from Our Own Wells

1. Helen Waddell, *The Desert Fathers*, 90.
2. Belden Lane, *Landscapes of the Sacred*, 229.
3. Belden Lane, *The Solace of Fierce Landscapes*, 3.
4. William Countryman, *The Poetic Imagination*, 18.
5. Gustavo Gutierrez, *We Drink from Our Own Wells*, 1984.
6. R. K. Narayan, "Such Perfection" in *Malgudi Days*, 64–67.
7. Awad Afifi, quoted in Lane, *The Solace of Fierce Landscapes*, 20–21.
8. Albert Raboteau, *A Fire in the Bones*, 137.
9. Martin Buber, *Tales of the Hasidim: Later Masters*, 249–50.
10. *The Cloud of Unknowing*, Chapter 65, Section 7.

Chapter 2: Feasting on the Word

1. Mark Reisler, "Always the Laborer, Never the Citizen: Anglo Perceptions of the Mexican Immigrant during the 1920s," 23–43.
2. Rabindranath Tagore, quoted in Ronald Takaki, *Strangers from a Different Shore*, 298.
3. *The Complete Poems of Emily Dickinson*, 506.
4. William Stringfellow, *An Ethic for Christians and Other Aliens in a Strange Land*, 13.
5. Robert McAfee Brown, *Unexpected News: Reading the Bible through Third World Eyes*.
6. Ronald Marstin, *Beyond our Tribal Gods*; Walter Brueggemann, *David's Truth in Israel's Imagination and Memory*.
7. *Symeon the New Theologian*, 170–71.
8. Naim Stifan Ateek, *Justice and Only Justice*, 77.
9. Midrash retold by Elizabeth Johnson, *She Who Is*, 260.
10. Robert Alter, *Canon and Creativity*, 77.
11. Robert Schreiter, *Constructing Local Theologies*.

12. Kosuke Koyama, *No Handle on the Cross*, 21.

13. Justo Gonzalez, *Mañana*, 75–78.

14. *The Bhagavad Gita*, 135, 146, 172. "Bhagavad Gita," which translates to "the Song of the Divine One," is a conversation between Krishna and Arjuna that elaborates on the Yogic teachings and blesses Arjuna with an awe-inspiring glimpse of Krishna's Absolute form.

Chapter 3: But Now I See

1. Annie Dillard, *For the Time Being*, 47.

2. Ralph Ellison, *Invisible Man*, 3.

3. James Baldwin, *Notes of a Native Son*, 93.

4. Gordon Allport, *The Nature of Prejudice*, 141.

5. Ibid., 3.

6. Yann Martell, *Life of Pi*, 64–70.

7. John Sayles, *Lone Star*.

8. Thich Nhat Hanh, *Living Buddha, Living Christ*, 184–85.

9. Takaki, *Strangers from a Distant Shore*, 396.

10. Tony Schwartz, "The Sounds of Evil," 144.

11. *A Keeper of the Word: Selected Writings of William Stringfellow*, 187–292.

12. William Stringfellow, *My People Is the Enemy*, 150.

13. Mohandas Gandhi, *Non-violent Resistance*, 210.

14. Martin Luther King Jr., *A Testament of Hope*, 569.

15. Thomas Merton, *The Wisdom of the Desert*, 8; *Gandhi on Non-violence*; 1–20; *The Nonviolent Alternative*, 253; *Contemplation in a World of Action*, 161.

16. Thomas Merton, *Contemplative Prayer*, 112.

17. Dorothy Day, *Meditations*, 62.

18. Donald Nicholl, *Holiness*, 42–44.

Chapter 4: Becoming Bread

1. Daniel C. Matt, *The Essential Kabbalah*, 134. *Kabbalah*

is an esoteric form of Jewish mysticism, which attempts to reveal hidden mystical insights in the Tanakh (Hebrew Bible).

2. Thomas Merton, *The Courage for Truth*, 89.
3. *Symeon the New Theologian*, 136–7, 369–70.
4. Dorotheos of Gaza, *Discourses and Sayings*, 138–39.
5. *The Dhammapada*, 43.
6. Day, *By Little and By Little*, 301.
7. Albert Camus, *The Fall*, 69–70.
8. Elie Wiesel, *The Town Beyond the Wall*, 159.
9. Jalal ad-Din Rumi, *Say I Am You*, 47.
10. Lester, *Ambassador of Reconciliation* 174.
11. Ibid., 157, 164.
12. Mohandas Gandhi, quoted in Walter Wink, *Peace Is the Way*, 162.
13. Adapted from Judith Palmer's article "Diversity: Three Paradigms."
14. Thich Nhat Hanh, *Touching Peace*, 45.
15. Frederick Douglass, *Life and Times of Frederick Douglass*, 151–52.
16. Jo Ann Ooiman Robinson, *Abraham Went Out: A Biography of A. J. Muste*, 130.
17. *Mahābhārata*, chapters 58–61. The *Mahābhārata* is one of the two major Sanskrit epics of ancient India, which includes the Bhagavad Gita, an important text of Hinduism.
18. Woody Allen, *Without Feathers*, 25.
19. John Bunyan, *The Pilgrim's Progress*, 285.
20. Matt, *The Essential Kabbalah*, 94–95.
21. *The Dhammapada*, 52.
22. *The Collected Works of St. John of the Cross*, 703.

Chapter 5: Rainbow Communities

1. King, Jr. *A Testament of Hope*, 21.
2. Desmond Tutu, *The Rainbow People of God*, 187–88.
3. For an account of the Koinonia community, see Tracy

Elaine K'Meyer, *The Story of Koinonia Farm: Interracialism and Christian Community in the Postwar South.*

4. Stringfellow, *An Ethic for Christians and Other Aliens in a Strange Land*, 61.

5. Wendell Berry, *The Hidden Wound*, 66.

6. Bernth Lindfors, *Conversations with Chinua Achebe*, 29, 137.

7. Thomas Merton, *The Silent Life*, 43.

8. Day, *By Little and By Little*, 85.

9. Thich Nhat Hanh, *Going Home*, 143.

10. Ibid., 98, 143, 177–81.

11. Kathleen Norris, *Amazing Grace*, 374.

12. R. S. Sugirtharajah, *Asian Biblical Hermeneutics and Postcolonialism*, 119.

13. Howard Thurman, *With Head and Heart*, 195.

14. Malcolm X, *The Autobiography of Malcolm X*, 323, 326, 336–7.

Epilogue

1. Shusaku Endo, *Deep River*, 107.

Bibliography

Allen, Woody. *Without Feathers*. New York: Random House, 1975.

Allport, Gordon. *The Nature of Prejudice*. Garden City, NY: Doubleday Anchor, 1954.

Alter, Robert. *Canon and Creativity: Modern Writing and the Authority of Scripture*. New Haven, CT: Yale University Press, 2000.

Ateek, Naim Stifan. *Justice and Only Justice: A Palestinian Theology of Liberation*. Maryknoll, NY: Orbis, 1990.

Baldwin, James. *Notes of a Native Son*. Boston: Beacon Press, 1955.

Berry, Wendell. *The Hidden Wound*. San Francisco: North Point Press, 1989.

Bhagavad Gita, The. Translated by Eknath Easwaran. Tomales, CA: Nilgiri Press, 1985.

Brown, Robert McAfee. *Unexpected News: Reading the Bible through Third World Eyes*. Louisville, KY: Westminster John Knox Press, 1984.

Brueggemann, Walter. *David's Truth in Israel's Imagination and Memory*. Philadelphia: Fortress Press, 1985.

Buber, Martin. *Tales of the Hasidim: Early Masters.* New York: Schocken Books, 1947.

———. *Tales of the Hasidim: Later Masters.* New York: Schocken Books, 1948.

Bunyan, John. *The Pilgrim's Progress.* New York: Books, Inc., 1945.

Camus, Albert. *The Fall.* New York: Vintage Books, 1956.

Climacus, John. *The Ladder of Divine Ascent.* New York: Paulist Press, 1982.

Cloud of Unknowing, The. Translated by Ira Progroff. New York: Dell Publishing, 1957.

Countryman, William. *The Poetic Imagination; An Anglican Spiritual Tradition.* Maryknoll, NY: Orbis, 1999.

Day, Dorothy. *On Pilgrimage.* New York: Catholic Worker Books, 1948.

———. *On Pilgrimage: The Sixties.* New York: Curtis Books, 1972.

———. *By Little and By Little: The Selected Writings of Dorothy Day.* Edited by Robert Ellsberg. New York: Alfred A. Knopf, 1983.

———. *Meditations.* Edited by Stanley Vishnewski. Mahwah, NJ: Paulist Press, 1970.

Dhammapada, The: The Path of Perfection. Translated by Juan Mascaro. New York: Penguin Classics, 1973.

Dickinson, Emily. *The Complete Poems of Emily Dickinson.* Edited by Thomas H. Johnson. Boston: Little, Brown and Company, 1960.

Dillard, Annie. *For the Time Being.* New York: Vintage Books, 1999.

Dorotheos of Gaza. *Discourses and Sayings.* Translated by Eric P. Wheeler. Kalamazoo, MI: Cistercian Publications, 1977.

Douglass, Frederick. *Life and Times of Frederick Douglass.* New York: Collier Books, 1962.

Ellison, Ralph. *Invisible Man.* New York: Vintage International, 1990.

Endo, Shusaku. *Deep River.* Translated by Van G. Gessel. New York: New Directions, 1994.

Erb, Peter C., ed. *Pietists: Selected Writings.* New York: Paulist Press, 1983.

Gandhi, Mohandas. *Non-violent Resistance.* New York: Schocken Books, 1951.

Gonzalez, Justo. *Mañana: Christian Theology from a Hispanic Perspective.* Nashville, TN: Abingdon, 1990.

Gutierrez, Gustavo. *We Drink from Our Own Wells: The Spiritual Journey of a People.* Maryknoll, NY: Orbis/Dove, 1984.

Hanh, Thich Nhat. *Going Home: Jesus and Buddha as Brothers.* New York: Riverhead Books, 1999.

———. *Living Buddha, Living Christ.* New York: Riverhead Books, 1995.

———. *Touching Peace: Practicing the Art of Mindful Living.* Berkeley, CA: Parallax Press, 1992.

John of the Cross. *The Collected Works of St. John of the Cross.* Translated by Kieran Kavanaugh and Otilio Rodriguez. Washington, DC: Institute of Carmelite Studies (ICS), 1979.

Johnson, Elizabeth. *She Who Is: The Mystery of God in Feminist Theological Discourse.* New York: Crossroad, 1992.

King, Martin Luther, Jr. *A Testament of Hope: The Essential Writings of Martin Luther King, Jr.* Edited by James Washington. San Francisco: Harper & Row, 1986.

K'Meyer, Tracy Elaine. *The Story of Koinonia Farm: Interracialism and Christian Community in the Postwar South.* Charlottesville, VA: University Press of Virginia, 1997.

Koyama, Kosuke. *No Handle on the Cross.* Maryknoll, NY: Orbis, 1977.

Lane, Belden. *Landscapes of the Sacred: Geography and*

Narrative in American Spirituality. Baltimore, MD: The Johns Hopkins University Press, 2001.

———. *The Solace of Fierce Landscapes.* New York: Oxford University Press, 1998.

Lester, Muriel. *Ambassador of Reconciliation: A Muriel Lester Reader.* Edited by Richard Deats. Philadelphia: New Society, 1991.

Lindfors, Bernth. *Conversations with Chinua Achebe.* Jackson, MS: University Press of Mississippi, 1997.

Macarius. *St. Macarius the Spiritbearer.* Translated by Tim Vivian. Crestwood, NY: St. Vladimir's Seminary Press, 2004.

Mahābhārata. Retold by Krishna Dharma. Badger, CA: Torchlight Publishing, 1999.

Malcolm X. *The Autobiography of Malcolm X.* New York: Grove Press, 1964.

Marstin, Ronald. *Beyond Our Tribal Gods: The Maturing of Faith.* Maryknoll, NY: Orbis, 1979.

Martell, Yann. *Life of Pi.* New York: Harcourt Brace, 2001.

Matt, Daniel C. *The Essential Kabbalah: The Heart of Jewish Mysticism.* San Francisco: HarperSanFrancisco, 1996.

Merton, Thomas. *Contemplation in a World of Action.* Garden City, NY: Doubleday Image, 1973.

———. *Contemplative Prayer.* Garden City, NY: Image, 1971.

———. *Gandhi on Non-Violence.* New York: New Directions, 1964.

———. *The Nonviolent Alternative.* New York: Farrar, Straus, and Giroux, 1971.

———. *The Silent Life.* New York: Farrar, Straus, and Giroux, 1957.

———. *The Wisdom of the Desert.* New York, New Directions, 1960.

———. *The Courage for Truth: Letters to Writers.* Selected and edited by Christine M. Bochen. New York: Harcourt Brace & Company, 1993.

————. *The Other Side of the Mountain: The Journals of Thomas Merton, Volume Seven 1967–1968.* Edited by Patrick Hart, O.C.S.O. New York: HarperSanFrancisco, 1998.

Muhammad. *The Wisdom of the Prophet: Sayings of Muhammad (Selections from the Hadith).* Translated by Thomas Cleary. Boston: Shambhala, 2001.

Muste, A. J. *The Essays of A. J. Muste.* Edited by Nat Hentoff. New York: Clarion, 1967.

Narayan, R. K. "Such Perfection" in *Malgudi Days.* London: Penguin, 1984.

Nicholl, Donald. *Holiness.* New York: Paulist Press, 1981.

Norris, Kathleen. *Amazing Grace: A Vocabulary of Faith.* New York: Riverhead Books, 1998.

————. *Dakota: A Spiritual Geography.* Boston: Mariner Books/Houghton Mifflin Company, 1993.

Palmer, Judith P. "Diversity: Three Paradigms." In *The Promise of Diversity*, edited by Judith H. Katz, Frederick A. Miller, Edith W. Seashore, and Elsie Y. Cross. New York: McGraw-Hill, 1994.

Raboteau, Albert. *A Fire in the Bones: Reflections on African-American Religious History.* Boston: Beacon Press, 1995.

Reisler, Mark. "Always the Laborer, Never the Citizen: Anglo Perceptions of the Mexican Immigrant during the 1920s" in *Between Two Worlds: Mexican Immigrants in the United States*, edited by David Gutierrez. Wilmington, DE: Jaguar Books, 1996.

Robinson, Jo Ann Ooimann. *Abraham Went Out: A Biography of A. J. Muste.* Philadelphia: Temple University Press, 1981.

Rumi, Jalāl ad-Dīn. *Say I Am You.* Translated by John Moyne and Coleman Barks. Athens, GA: Maypop, 1994.

Sayles, John. *Lone Star.* Sony Picture Classics, 1996.

Schreiter, Robert. *Constructing Local Theologies.* Maryknoll, NY: Orbis, 1986.

Schwartz, Tony. "The Sounds of Evil." In *Facing Evil*, edited by Paul Woodruff and Harry A. Wilmer. LaSalle, IL: Open Court, 1988.

Stringfellow, William. *An Ethic for Christians and Other Aliens in a Strange Land.* Waco, TX: Word Books, 1973.

———. *My People is the Enemy: An Autobiographical Polemic.* Garden City, NY: Doubleday Anchor, 1964.

———. *A Keeper of the Word; Selected Writings of William Stringfellow.* Edited by Bill Wylie Kellermann. Grand Rapids, MI: William B. Eerdmans, 1994.

Sugirtharajah, R. S. *Asian Biblical Hermeneutics and Post-colonialism: Contesting the Interpretations.* Maryknoll, NY: Orbis, 1998.

Symeon. *Symeon the New Theologian: The Discourses.* Translated by C. J. DeCatanzaro. New York, Paulist Press, 1980.

Takaki, Ronald. *Strangers from a Different Shore: A History of Asian Americans.* New York: Penguin, 1989.

Thurman, Howard. *With Head and Heart: The Autobiography of Howard Thurman.* New York: Harcourt Brace, 1979.

Tutu, Desmond. *The Rainbow People of God: The Making of a Peaceful Revolution.* New York: Doubleday, 1994.

Waddell, Helen. *The Desert Fathers.* Ann Arbor, MI: University of Michigan Press, 1957.

Wiesel, Elie. *The Town Beyond the Wall.* New York: Avon, 1964.

Wink, Walter. *Peace Is the Way: Writings on Nonviolence from the Fellowship of Reconciliation.* Maryknoll, NY: Orbis, 2000.